Super Moms, Inc.:

Work From Home, Build A Profitable Home Business, And Find Time For Your Family When You Have Kids To Take Care Of!

Carolyn Woods

Contents

Introduction

My Story

This story starts a little over 12 years ago, when my daughter was born. I had worked 100% travel jobs for years, but just couldn't go back to that once my bundle of joy came home from the hospital. I interviewed for a few new positions, but they all required travel and I just wasn't willing!

At that point, I decided it was time to figure out a way to pay the bills without a traditional job. Twelve plus years after this story started, I have four kids, own a home, and am able to support my family while working part time out of my house.

I still remember the huge relief when my oldest child got the chicken pox at 11 months old and I didn't have to call and explain to an angry boss why I wasn't going to come into work for the next 10 days. I was already working from home, so it wasn't a big impact on anyone! When my twins were born I had large medical bills to pay off since my insurance didn't cover anything to do with pregnancy or delivery, so I hired a full time nanny who helped with the babies and ran errands and I worked full time consulting from the house for a couple of years to pay everything off. Then I cut back on my schedule, so I could be available to take the kids back and forth to school myself. A little later, one of my children needed to be pulled out of school and I cut my work schedule way back so I could spend time with him and be available for his many appointments during the week. As I write this, all of my kids are home for a school break and I've adjusted my schedule so I get most of my work done early in the morning, while they wake up and watch a TV show. Then I'm available for fun the rest of the day!

How to Use This Book

This book is divided into two main sections: Developing Your Plan, and Designing Your Business.

In "Developing Your Plan", we'll talk about some different aspects of starting up your business, including the option of a traditional job and ways to reduce expenses. There are also some worksheets to help you map out your personal business plan.

You may be wondering why I include a discussion of expenses. Keep in mind that a business can take weeks or months to ramp up, so if you can give yourself some time to get rolling without financial panic, that is good! Anything you can do ahead of time to save, reduce ongoing expenses, and delay new purchases is good during this initial period. If you feel less financial pressure, you can keep your focus on building a business, rather than worrying where your next check is coming from.

I've also included a chapter on emergency cash flow, which are things you can do if you have a gap in income you need to cover. Unfortunately, these are emergency methods, so you won't be able to make them work for very long or very often but they can help you through a rough patch when you need them.

The "Designing Your Business" section will cover many ways to earn money while keeping your kids as your first priority. All of them have been done, either by me or by someone I know, so they come with real world proof that they are viable (unlike some of the Internet-based opportunities out there!). Some of the options will allow you to work from home or to take the kids along and some will require some kid-free time, such as during school or via some sort of childcare program, swap, or arrangement with friends or family.

Use these ideas as a starting point. You can combine multiple ideas with your strengths and skills, and come up with a unique business that perfectly suits you!

Getting Your Business Going

It takes time and focus to get a business started, so I'd recommend you read this guide, list out some options, and then pick one to start with and give it your full attention. Once it has some momentum you can add on other activities, one at a time. If you spread your focus too far nothing will happen! Instead, think of this like building a skyscraper. You need the first level to be stable before you start adding on to your building, so make sure it's secure before you divert attention to the next level.

Please don't skip the section on determining how much income you really need, and the discussion on ways to reduce your needs because reduced expenses means less time working, and more time for your family! Once you have your parameters, read on to the chapters with specific ideas you can implement to develop your own personal home business plan.

Now, grab some paper or a laptop to make notes, and let's get started!

Developing Your Plan

1

What About A Traditional Job?

When moms want to work out of the house one of the first things they often do is start looking for a traditional home-based or part time job. While this sounds easy since you've probably been out in the regular job market for years, the legitimate home-based positions are competitive and the scams are rampant. However, if you feel this might be the right opportunity for you, read on and I'll talk about how to find the legitimate positions out there.

First, here are the pros and cons I've come up with for taking a traditional job:

Pros:

- Regular pay and taxes taken out.
- No ramp up period, you receive your set amount of pay right away.
- Similar to having a traditional office job, so you have specific hours to be available and materials you need to complete your job.

Cons:

- Generally not very flexible in terms of hours, and timing of those hours
- Some people find working out of their house too lonely, or have trouble staying organized and focused when surrounded by dishes that need washing and other household chores not yet completed.

A traditional position may make a lot of sense since it allows for more time with the family without having to start up a business ourselves. The dark side is that you need to work within that job's requirements, which may or may not fit with your own. I'd encourage you to start with the "Making Your Plan" chapter in this book first. Put together the income and lifestyle that will work best for your family. Then when you locate a traditional job opportunity, you can see how well it fits into the lifestyle you're in the process of creating. It might be too structured, or too few hours, or require an occasional evening, which you don't want to do. Or, it might be the cornerstone of your new and improved lifestyle, fitting into the time of day and situation where you're available and filling in one of your income blocks perfectly.

Here are suggested steps to take to locate a traditional part time or home-based position:

Talking to your current employer

If you have a position you'd be willing to continue doing if you could do it from home (at least some of the time) or on a part time basis, talk to you current employer before you do anything else. The people who already know you will be more likely to work with you on a modified position than those who don't.

Set up a meeting with your boss, and walk in with a proposal of how it could work. You'll need to include the hours you'll work (when will you be available? Will you still work full time or do you want to cut back? Do you have a suggestion for a job share or other creative option?), your responsibilities (are there any you won't be able to do from offsite? Will you still show up for staff meetings or other regular events?), and your compensation (will it change?). Present your suggestions, but don't be upset if they say no or need time to think about it. Once they've had some time they may come back to you with a yes or a modified plan. Remember that you can always build a business on the side or look for a new telecommute position if this one doesn't work out, so keep a good attitude while trying to negotiate with your current employer.

Finding Legitimate Jobs Online

There are a great many websites out there offering information on "legitimate" home-based positions, most of them with a directory you can purchase for a fee.

However, experience tells me that:

- Most part time jobs are built around a specific need or person, rather than being always available. To find these positions, your best bet is for a friend or recruiter to refer you to the hiring company. Sign up with recruiters in your area (remember, legitimate recruiters will not charge you a fee!) and make sure all your friends know you're in the market, so they'll know to recommend you should the opportunity arise.

- Legitimate jobs will usually advertise through the regular job sites or recruiters. Spend your time on the big job sites like Monster (http://www.monster.com/), Indeed (http://www.indeed.com/), CareerBuilder (http://www.careerbuilder.com/), and local job sites like Craigslist (http://www.craigslist.org).

Chapter Summary

Legitimate part time and home-based jobs are out there, but it's a pretty small portion of the market so you'll likely need some patience.

To locate a part time or home-based position, first talk to you current employer (if you have one) to see if they'll adjust your current job to suit your new needs. If that doesn't work out, focus on the large online job boards rather than buying a directory online.

2

Things That Didn't Work

In my 12 years of being a work at home mom, I've tried a LOT of different options to make money. Here are some of my failures - this certainly doesn't mean no one makes money from these, but I feel like I gave them a good chance and none of them covered my costs.

Direct Sales and Party Sales Plans

I believe just about everyone I know has tried one of the party sales plans at least once, and of all the people I've talked to about them, I only know of one person who actually makes a reasonable income from it (she says $1,000 to $2,000 a month, and she does a few parties each week). For me, this success rate (1 out of a whole bunch!) doesn't meet the "good business to get into" criteria. However, they are popular - great products, sounds like it would be easy, and lots of options! Understand that I can't recommend these unless you just want to buy a lot of their products and are using this to get a good discount.

For those who are going to try it anyway, I did a series of interviews with moms who sell via these plans a few years back. Here's a summary of what I learned:

1. In most cases, you must buy a starter kit, which contains some selling materials and product samples. The price ranges from $100 - $300.
2. You book parties or sell products and earn a commission on the results. If the products sell through parties, your key to success is obtaining bookings for additional parties at each event. (Interviewees said that generous hostess gifts is a huge advantage in this). If you sell directly, your key to success is to sell to more people or more products to current customers (excellent follow up and a consumable product are good strategies here), plus you are generally paid a commission on sales by reps who sign up under you (so you also want to develop your recruiting skills).
3. Many of these programs have monthly minimum sales amounts, which you must meet to remain a rep.
4. Some of these programs have ongoing monthly fees, such as for a website.
5. Many of these programs have restrictions on the way you market or sell your product, such as places you can sell (no online auctions is a common one).
6. Some programs don't want you to work for other plans. However you may want to have more than one program (assuming you can meet the monthly minimums) to have more reasons to keep in touch with your customers. (for example: if you sell party supplies to a customer, they may also need a party gift, plus they

may need gifts for other parties they attend throughout the year. You have the chance to increase your sales, and by keeping in touch with them to see if they need gifts, you may get referrals for others who need party supplies).

Still sounds interesting? Here is a list of questions to run through before you select the company you're going to work with, to make sure it's the best choice for you:

1. Are you passionate about the product? Will you enjoy it?
2. Are there quotas or territories imposed?
3. What is the cost to get started? Is there a kit? Do you have to buy business aids and an inventory? Can you earn the starter kits or bonus inventory when you start? How much time and money do you have to invest before you see a profit?
4. How do you place orders? How does the commission scale work? Do you have to place minimum orders to get full commission or do you receive it on small orders also? Can you only place orders of certain volume? Can you place orders online, by phone or fax? How is the sales support? Can you place orders any day of the month or must you wait for campaigns to end?
5. Inventory - Do you have to keep one?
6. What are the incentives? This is the fun stuff! What do you have to do to earn free products each month? What quality are they? Are they things you can apply to your business? Are the trips and reward programs available to everyone at all levels?
7. Is there a rewards program for the hostess? Will a hostess want to book with you? Is it valuable? Who pays for it?
8. What is the compensation plan? Can you earn a living as a new consultant with right now money? What do you

have to do to reach the next level? How much more do you earn as your level in management increases? How soon do you start earning residual income and bonuses? Do you have any quotas or minimums? How and when do you receive the commission?

9. What is the company's information? How long has the company been in business? What is its record with the BBB? Is it a member of the Direct Selling Assoc.? Is the company debt free? What is their annual/quarterly percentage of growth? Is your area saturated with reps or is there room to advance and offer a unique service? How many consultants/sales reps are in the country? How many consultants/sales reps are in the local area? What were the gross sales for the last 2 years and what are the projected sales for this year?

10. Are the products unique and consumable? Are they good quality? Will you use them and love them? What is the supply and demand?

11. What is your upline? How long has your sponsor been in the business? Has he/she had success? How committed are they to their business and to your success? Are there meetings or conference calls you can attend? What is the training like? Does she have a duplicatable system in place? Is it successful?

12. Is there good training and corporate support? The last thing you want is to feel like you've been left in the dark when starting a new business.

13. Is the party simple and duplicatable? With a short and simple presentation, your audience is captured, not bored. Your sales increase because they stick around for the entire presentation and your sponsoring increases because they watch and think, "This is easy, I can do this too!"

14. Do you make the deliveries or do they ship to the hostess?

15. What monthly fees do you have?

16. What things are free? Think about Web pages, supplies, forms, newsletters, online order placing, and use of company websites.
17. Do you have to have a credit card, debit card, or checking account to join?
18. Do you have to attend meetings or rally?
19. How much does the average consultant sell in one month? How many hours of work does it take to earn the average number of sales per month?
20. How can you market your home business? Can you place ads in local or national papers or magazines? Can you promote or advertise on the Internet? Can you do "Cash & Carry" sales at expos, fairs, or shows? Can you make my own materials, such as flyers and business cards? (This will save you tons of money if you can.) Can you make your own website, or must you pay for a website through the company? Are individual websites available? If so, what is the cost? Does the company provide or sell marketing products such as catalogs, business cards, magnetic car signs, etc.?
21. Can you sell products from another Direct Sales company?
22. Does the company stand behind its products? Is there a return policy?
23. How many levels are paid out?
24. Are there local training meetings or are you left on your own to fend for yourself?
25. What is included in your initial kit? Can you shrink or enlarge the kit (and change your initial investment)?

Remember, if you were going to a job, you would never have to pay them to work for them, so don't take a job where you have to pay every month to work or to join! It is one thing to get a kit or products to show, like with most of the plans out there, but don't fall for any scams!

Websites, Blogging, and Newsletters

I lump these together because they all generate income from commissions on product sales or referrals.

There are many guides to this type of business available on the Internet (most for a price!). Here is a summary of the basic program:

1. Select a theme or topic for your site or blog. Ideally, it's something that you have expertise and interest in, and where there is a fair amount of interest in, as based on Internet searches. To figure out the number of searches, use the Google AdWords keyword tool, currently at https://adwords.google.com/. Look for the "Get Keyword Ideas" link and click on it. There is no need to sign in to use this.

To use the tool:

> In the top box for "word or phrase", type in words or phrases relating to your key topic to figure out which have the most searches. For example, for a website on the same topic as this book, I might have typed "work at home" and "home business". Each search phrase or term goes on a separate line, so hit the enter key in between them. Type in the spam checker info, then click on "search".

> To come up with the best words or phrases for your site, put yourself in the buyer's shoes. If they really wanted a book exactly like yours, what sort of things would they search for to try to find it? Once you find a

few search terms that fit with your book and have a high number of searches, you have found it!

At the lower part of your screen, you will see each of your words and phrases and the number of monthly searches for each. This will allow you to optimize your title based on the key words most often used to look for information on the subject you're writing about.

2. Set up a site or blog on the topic you've selected from your research. You will want to use your keywords in your site address and/ or blog name. Google treats a hyphen like a space, so feel free to use hyphens in your name. For example, if your key words are "Learn Spanish Fast", you will want to set up a site with the address learn-spanish-fast.com. Since you will be mostly bringing people in via clickable links, go longer if you have to to get an address with your keywords. If learn-spanish-fast.com isn't available, you might end up with learn-to-speak-spanish-fast-and-easy.com instead.

3. Write a bunch of pages (say 20+) or regular (most say at least weekly) blog posts with lots of "meat" that provides outstanding information for folks who are interested in the topic. Or do both - the ideal situation is a "meaty" site which gets lots of search engine traffic combined with a newsletter signup box on every page. Once your visitors sign up for your newsletter or blog, you can keep in touch with them and send them ongoing information on the topic.

4. Include occasional links to products or sites that you recommend as high quality on your site or in your posts. Be sure the products or sites are ones that you believe are helpful or will be of interest to your target audience, or that you receive a commission or affiliate fee for when purchases are made.

5. Focus on building traffic (which should be easy due to your high quality content - though there are a lot of competitors out there!), and as your traffic and readership grows so will your sales and your income.

Sounds simple right? I suspect for some people it is, but personally I've not found that I had it in me to keep coming up with informative high quality posts week after week for minimal money in (my high earnings for a week was probably under $100). If you are an excellent writer and have a topic you're passionate about, this could be an excellent option but for most of us, not so much.

Chapter Summary

There are many great business opportunities out there, but here are a couple of common ones I feel are not so great:

- Party plan sales

- Information-based website or blog

These may be awesome opportunities if you want results from them that aren't strictly income-based - buying products for a discount, or meeting others passionate about your passion - but personally I haven't found them to provide a return on my efforts.

3

Get Those Expenses Down!

I know some of you are rolling your eyes at this point, thinking that this book is supposed to be about making money, not spending less! If your partner's income fully supports your family and you are looking for some extra cash to fund an exotic vacation, you can definitely skip this part. But most of us have some amount of financial pressure, and if you can reduce your expenses that pressure lightens up. In my case, I'm the sole support of my four children, and reducing expenses was the only way I could free up time to spend with them.

Many of your situations will be somewhere in the middle of these two scenarios, but you'll likely find that focusing less on "stuff" and more on time with the family will make your life happier. One of the easiest ways to do that is to reduce what you need, so that you don't need as much time working to pay for those needs. Reducing what you spend can take a lot of pressure off you in the early stages of your business building, and may even change your goals.

To get started, add up everything you've spent for the past few months, so you know what's really going out the door (as opposed to the minimum amounts you probably carry in your head). Then, examine each area and see if you can reduce it. You'll have the motivation of reaching your goals quicker.

Here's a worksheet you can fill out with your current expenses. Fill in the month in the first column, and some broad categories of expenses in the second column. Add up what you spent in each category for the last month, and fill in the "$ Spent" column with those totals. Make sure it totals up to the amount you spent for each month, so you are sure you included everything.

Month	Expenditure Type	$ Spent	$ Target
Total for month:			

Once you know where your income is going, read the rest of the chapter and come up with some ideas to reduce your expenditures going forward. Then, come up with a target for each area and fill in the final column with it.

In future months, fill in the first three columns with your actual expenditures, and put those targets in the 4th column. Then, evaluate each area and see how you are doing. If you're not meeting your targets you may need to change them, or you may need to come up with some new actions to reduce your monthly spending to reach them.

This tracking can be easier if you use a tool like Quicken. It will link up to most banks and credit cards and download your spending automatically. If you enter a budget into the program, you can print out a report at the end of the month instead of adding everything up.

Here are ideas to help reduce many common expenses:

Mortgage

It's probably worth a call to your local banker if you've had the same loan for more than a couple of years to see if they can save you some money with a lower interest rate. Rates and programs change constantly and you may be able to save some money each month with a small amount of effort.

Utilities

A basic level of utilities is required, but you have a lot of latitude above that. Do you have a timer on your thermostat so your heater or air conditioner isn't working as hard when everyone is out? Can you save some money on services from the cable company by reducing your features or buying one of the bundled plans? I know I have a combination telephone/long distance/ cable TV/Internet plan that is quite a bit less than purchasing the services individually. You may be able to change your watering schedule or even replace some grass with an alternative look and reduce your monthly water bill.

Groceries

This is one of the most controllable areas of spending.

I've read many guides to using coupons and seen the extreme examples of what can be done with a lot of planning, but my experience was that the main benefit of coupons was to allow me to purchase brand name items for the same price as the off brand That wasn't worth the time to me.

Instead, I keep a log of grocery prices for things I regularly buy in a notebook. I have to tell you that when I first heard this idea, I thought it sounded way too structured and silly for me, but it's been a great help. When I spot a sale that sounds good, I check my book to make sure I'm not being tricked! Then when I find a really good deal, I know it. I watch grocery ads for sales on more expensive items like meat, and after checking my book to make sure it's a great deal, I'll buy large quantities while it's a bargain. I can portion meat out into single meal servings in Ziploc bags and put them in the freezer so I can easily get one out in the morning to thaw for dinner.

I buy seasonal produce so the prices are low, and buy very little processed food. To my surprise, I found that it takes me just a few more minutes to make things like muffins from scratch vs. prepared from a mix and that the price was about half. The savings on making my own chicken piccata (as it turns out, it only has five ingredients) vs. the big box of premade at Sam's Club was much more extreme, and I had the option of making it more healthy (using chicken pieces I could identify and less butter). Making my own pizza crust takes about 15 minutes and an hour to rise - and I make a recipe of enough for 8 pizzas. It freezes great, and we can thaw out a bag of pizza crust dough any time we want homemade pizza.

I also make larger meals and freeze leftovers so I don't have to cook every night. I "repackage" things like leftover chicken into burritos or enchiladas so it doesn't feel like we've having the same meal over and over.

My kids went through a stage of wanting to be vegetarian, and through that, we discovered a lot of healthy and economical bean-based dishes that we eat pretty regularly now.

You can have some fun with it! My kids just love to get Happy Meals from McDonalds. They don't even seem to like the food or toys much, it's just the novelty. So once in a while I'll surprise them with our homemade version! We have some lunch bags we hang on to that say "happy meal" with a smiley face on them (or you could even keep the bags from some real Happy Meals for this). I made little french fry holders out of stapled paper, and cook some frozen french fries to fill them. Then I make turkey burgers or chicken nuggets, cut up an apple, and drop in a small surprise of some sort... voila! Instant entertainment!

Household Items

The very first question here is, do you really need it? If so, do you need it now? Delay things if you can. If not, then shop around to make sure you get a good deal, and take some time to watch for special bargains. You can purchase many items used but in good condition; this may make sense depending on the item and how much you use it.

Outings and Activities

Gas can be expensive these days, so planning outings that you can walk to or carpooling with a friend can mean savings. I've found that with four kids, local memberships are a bargain - a family membership at the children's museum was the same as the cost of two visits, and my planetarium membership gave us access to their educational movies (which are short enough that my kids don't get restless like they do in the theater) year round for free. Take a look at the activities your family enjoys and see if you can change them or bulk purchase to save some bucks.

Preschool, Daycare, and School

The best way to save money on daycare or preschool is simply to not have your children attend! If you do need the child-free time or feel that the skills they'll learn in preschool are important, look around to make sure you've found the most appropriate program in terms of the times they are available, the skills they will teach and the price they charge. For example, you may find another mom with a preschool background who is happy to teach your toddlers along with her own, for a fraction of the childcare center rate. If you mostly need child-free time, you may be able to arrange for care with another mom, or even a swap where you each get two days a week child-free. If you feel an organized program is the best answer, talk to them about their pricing as some have some flexibility to offer you discounts.

Kids' Clothing

I personally like to buy my kids' clothes from Gymboree and Hanna Andersson. I think they're cute and excellent quality, and they still look good after lots of wear. I used to purchase most of my kids clothing from their websites, getting my favorites when they came out and stocking up on basics during sales.

When I went into "frugal mode", I realized I needed to change my strategy. I considered switching to inexpensive items from Old Navy and Wal-Mart, but I found they didn't last as long and were much more likely to hold stains, get holes, etc.

So I came up with a completely new strategy. This may or may not work for you. I started watching for lots of used brand name clothing in my kids' sizes on craigslist.org. These would be from local people who shopped at the stores I liked, and I generally found that the prices were reasonable (less than eBay for previously worn items). Once I found items in good condition, I'd buy them - often the whole batch, after negotiating a discount.

We'd try on the items, and decide which specifically we wanted to keep. Then, any outgrown and still nice clothes plus any newly purchased items that we didn't want, I'd sell on eBay. My spending on kids' clothes after deducting what I sold them for was comparable to shopping at Wal-Mart, but we got to wear much higher quality stuff.

You definitely need to factor your time to shop and resell in a strategy like this, but the point is that there are many ways to achieve a particular result, once you know what it is!

It may be that you just can't work with used items, but you could still limit your purchases, stick to the sales, keep things in nice condition and resell them at the end.

Another strategy is to set up a clothes exchange or hand-me-down train with people you know. For example, at one point I gave my older daughter's outgrown clothing to another family (there are eight years between my girls, and I don't have space to store things that long) in exchange for their outgrown boy clothing, which was large enough for my older boy, and could be handed down to the younger one. I also had two friends who gave me all their outgrown items for years, which was perfect for my younger daughter.

Another fun option is to get a group together - could be friends or people you know through another organization like a mom's group or school - for a clothing swap. You can set parameters, such as specific sizes and genders, which are applicable for the attendees. Everyone brings a bag of clothing and you dump them all out and sort into some basic piles by gender/size. Then, everyone goes through the items there and takes home what they can use.

Feeling Extreme?

Some people may decide to take more drastic measures to reduce their expenses, to either extensively reduce their need for income to do more things with their children. Perhaps you have a sick child, or a budding gymnast who needs to travel to events during the week, or need more time to homeschool, or due to life circumstances that they aren't able to change at the moment (job loss, divorce, death of a spouse, illness). If you're in that category, here are some additional options to consider:

- share your space: take in a roommate, rent a room in someone else's home, or rent a larger home or apartment with another family

- go smaller: move into an apartment/smaller apartment or trailer

- go rural: move further out of town, where rents and housing prices are much lower. This also may give you the opportunity to grow or raise some of your own food to reduce your expenses further.

- take a job with room and board: the most likely scenario for this is a live-in nanny position. Some employers will allow you to bring one child along. This probably isn't an option if you are married/living with someone or have multiple children.

- accept government assistance: if your income is low enough, you may also qualify for food stamps and Medicaid, which can further reduce your expenses for groceries and (if you have it now) medical insurance.

- watch for free: many items can be obtained free on freecycle.com or in the free section of craigslist.org. I know I personally have given away a washer and dryer, kids' clothing and furniture.

Chapter Summary

You need to know your income needs before you can plan your income strategy, so start by looking at your spending. Any reductions in spending mean less income needed, which can be a big stress reducer when you are starting up a business from scratch. Reductions also mean less time needed for work, which leaves more time for everything else!

4

Your Income Plan

This will get a little more fun now. In this section, you'll figure out what you're going to do to bring in income and how you'll make it fit with your goals and lifestyle. By the time you're finished, you should have a road map showing your desired goal and how you plan to reach it.

Developing Your Goals

The first thing I encourage you to do in your quest for generating money from home is to write down your goals. You wouldn't go on a long trip without looking at a map and this is a similar scenario. You're putting a long range series of activities in place and you need to know where you're going and why you're doing them.

Start with why you want to do this. You might have a specific, limited goal, like saving for a vacation or a large purchase. You might want to supplement your family's income with a little extra each month, to cover unexpected expenses or fun outings. You might have a larger goal, like quitting your current position and staying home full time with your kids. In my case, I'm a single parent and wanted to work from home and generate enough income to support my family while still having some time to spend with them!

Once you have your goal, you need to quantify exactly how much money you need to generate to meet it.

Don't forget to keep track of your other goals. For instance, one of my goals was to finish work by the time my kids came home from school, so I could focus on them - helping with homework, fixing a healthy dinner, and sitting down with them to catch up on events from school. I had to modify my income goal so that I could cover my expenses and still be signing off my computer by 3pm. One thing I had to do was to "fire" a lucrative but high maintenance client. Although the income was nice to have, the client often sent large projects with a short turnaround which required working evenings and weekends to keep up, and receiving calls at home in the evening.

Focus

If you try to do too many things all at once, you won't be able to do any of them very well. When you're developing your plan, make sure you give yourself time to focus on a single business until it's up and running. Once that first piece is in place, spend some of your free time bringing piece #2 online. Don't add more to your plate until the two income pieces you're working on are both running pretty smoothly. If you start #2 and #1 falls apart, you aren't really getting ahead! Give yourself some time to get everything settled in before you change what you're doing.

Work Time

You'll need to think carefully about the work time you have available. If your children are in school, you may have several hours available on school days, but no time when school is closed, so you need to select options that don't require an ongoing daily commitment from you. Perhaps selling online or writing a book would meet your schedule.

Some of you have small children and want to work out of the home or out of a place where you can bring them with you, for just an hour or two a day. Perhaps you can combine dog walking with a trip to the park or scooter around the block for them, or can be available as a virtual assistant for two hours each afternoon during naptime.

Evening activities, such as teaching, might be possible if you have a spouse or neighbor (or even an older child) who can watch your children while you're out.

If you give lessons or tutoring at your home, your children may be able to play quietly, watch TV, or even join in for group activities.

Selecting Your Income Generators

Now the fun part! Come up with a short list of income generators you think will work for you. You can start with a brainstorming process or read section two of this book to get some ideas. Once you have your short list, you'll need to do some research to figure out what you can charge for the business or how much you'll make on the markup for your area. After you've calculated some rates, use them to fill in the matrix below to make sure your plan will help you reach your objectives.

Here are two ways of brainstorming:

1. Mind Map

In a mind map, you start with a word or phrase in the middle of the page. In this situation, it might be "Ways to Generate Income" or "Skills I Have That Might Work With a Home Business". Put a circle around it. Then, as you think of ideas, draw a line from the circle out and write the idea. When you come up with a new idea, give it its own line if it's different; if it's related to an existing one, then write it near that one. Keep going as long as you can to generate many ideas. Don't judge anything as silly or not useful at this point; even a silly idea may lead you to something fantastic later.

Here's a sample of a mind map. Note that the ring of circles closest to the center theme of "Ideas" are skills or interest, and the branches out from them are specific ways we might use those skills or interests.

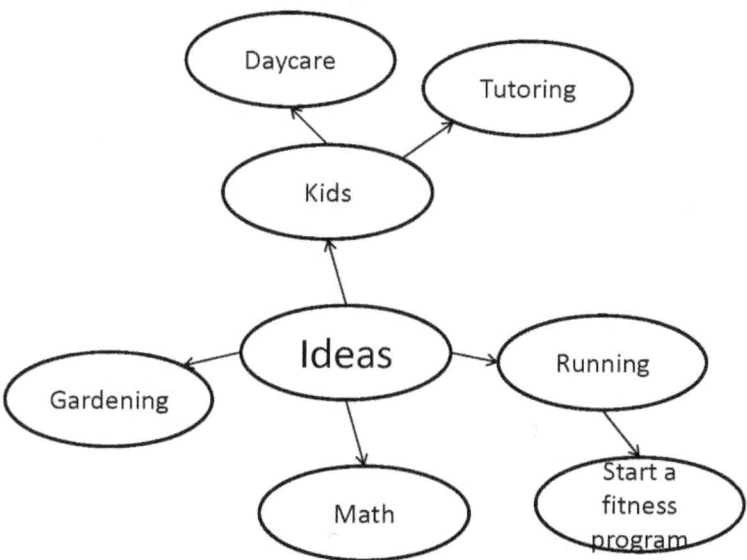

Once you're finished, you'll have a lot of ideas you can further evaluate. You may notice a lot of your ideas cluster around one or two main ideas. These are likely main branches to use going forward, since you obviously already have skills and interests in those areas.

2. List of Strengths and Ideas

Another way to generate potential business ideas is by developing a list of your skills, strengths, and things that you enjoy. Go through and review them to see what business ideas you can come up with that utilize your strengths and things you already like to do. Here's an example:

Strengths	Skills	Things I Enjoy
Helping others understand difficult concepts	Teaching - especially toddlers Organized	Being outside Doing activities with my kids Learning new things

In this example, we might combine "Helping others understand difficult concepts" + "Teaching toddlers" + "Organized" + "Doing activities with my kids" and come up with "Teach preschoolers to read" or "Teach sports skills to kids at the park, including mine"!

Here's a matrix you can start from:

Strengths	Skills	Things I Enjoy

Next, circle the seven or eight items that you feel most strongly about in the above list. Each one of them can be useful for brainstorming some ideas on how you might generate income from them.

To use this worksheet, put one of your starred items at the top of the page. Then, think of ways you might be able to use that in a business. Don't judge anything now - silly is OK, since a silly idea might later be the inspiration you need to come up with a usable one!

Strength, Skill or Thing I Enjoy:

_____

Ways I might be able to use this:

1.
2.
3.
4.
5.
6.
7.
8.
9.
10.

Income From Your Ideas

Now that you have a list of potential business options, you need to come up with some idea of what you could charge for these services or goods so that you can see how well each business would fit with your objectives. Please don't immediately rule out something you think you'd enjoy for income reasons since your choice may depend on the hours needed, time of day you have available to work, necessity for days off, flexibility, and ability to bring your kids along, along with the rate per job or hour. Something that initially looks promising might require an expensive babysitter or more time away than you have available and something less lucrative but more flexible might end up meeting your income needs just fine - and be fun for you as well! Take the time to analyze all your great ideas before you start ruling them out.

To figure out what you could charge, locate similar businesses online. Many will give rates for services on their website; others will require a phone call to get pricing. Put together a list of your research results, and use them to estimate what you could charge in your area for the service or product.

Keep track of your research; you'll need it in the next step:

Business Idea	What I Think I Can Charge

The Work Income Matrix

As you pull together this information, fill out a work income matrix and make sure it seems realistic to you. In many cases, it will take some time to ramp up your target income. However, if you need to generate $500 a week and only have 10 hours available, it is still doable. Figure you can manage two dog walks a day, five days a week. At $10 per dog and with five dogs in your group, that is two walks x five days = 10 walks a week. Five dogs x $10=$50 per walk, or 10 walks x $50 per walk=$500 per week. That is a realistic goal! The same target income goal with only five hours available would not be workable, as that would only generate $250 per week. So in the latter case, you'd need to increase your available work hours come up with a business that you could commit more hours to (perhaps out of your home rather than traveling from place to place), or develop another plan that would provide higher rates.

To use the matrix, fill in each square where you have work time available with the amount of time you can generally commit. Then, as you select income-generating methods for your different situations, you will come back, fill in the position, and calculate the expected income generated in that timeframe. You'll also note any related expenses. For example, when I teach in the evenings, I have to hire a babysitter, which I wouldn't otherwise need. That goes in the "Related Expenses" row so I know how much income I actually generate toward my goals. Once it's complete, you can add up the expected income and see if it meets your goals.

Here's an example, based on our dog walking example above:

	Mon	Tues	Wed	Thurs	Fri
Morning	2 hours. 2 dogs walks, 5 dogs per session, $10 per dog = $100	2 hours. 2 dogs walks, 5 dogs per session, $10 per dog = $100	2 hours. 2 dogs walks, 5 dogs per session, $10 per dog = $100	2 hours. 2 dogs walks, 5 dogs per session, $10 per dog = $100	2 hours. 2 dogs walks, 5 dogs per session, $10 per dog = $100
Afternoon					
Evening					
Total time and income	2 hours, $100	2 hours, $100	2 hours, $100	2 hours, $100	2 hours, $100
Related expenses					
Ending time and income	2 hours, $100	2 hours, $100	2 hours, $100	2 hours, $100	2 hours, $100

Total for the week: 2 hours in the morning, Monday through Friday, $500 per week.

Here's a blank matrix you can fill out:

	Mon	Tues	Wed	Thurs	Fri	Sat	Sun
Morning							
Afternoon							
Evening							
Total time and income							
Related Expenses							
Ending time and Income							

Total time and income: _____

Developing Your Goals and Timeline

Once you've selected a business to proceed with, write up a list of all the steps you need to take to make it a reality. Then, assign a completion date next to each one. Keep this list next to your computer or in a visible spot in your kitchen, and try to take action on something on your list every day so you keep moving toward your goal.

Here's a chart you can use to list out those tasks and keep track of their status:

Task	Complete by	Date completed

Chapter Summary:

- Planning is an important step in the process. Before your devote your time to building a business, think through the entire process and make sure your expectations about the time you'll need to devote to it and the income you'll earn are realistic. You don't want to be six months down the road with a significant investment of effort and realize you aren't getting closer to your goals, or are even losing ground each month!

- Start with the amount of money you have to make and the time you have available and be sure whatever your plan is, it is capable of generating the income you need in the time you have. If not, you'll need to change the income needed, the time available or the business itself.

- Once you've found a business idea you're excited about and which has the potential to meet your goals - develop a detailed list of what you need to do to get it started and take some action every day!

5

Emergency Measures

When you're starting up your own business, it is possible that you will have times of low or even no cash flow and need to implement some emergency cash measures. Here are some ideas in case you run into that situation.

To generate cash quickly, you will want to look at two possibilities: in-person sales and personal services.

In-Person Sales:

By "in-person sales", I mean a situation where you hand the purchased item to the buyer and they need to pay you right away. The most common example of this would be a garage sale. Garage sales work best in the summer, but an emergency garage sale can work most any day or time. A potentially easier way to handle this situation would be a posting on craigslist (http://www.craigslist.org) if you have one for your area. You can resale children's items at consignment stores. You can also try reselling gift cards for a percentage of their face value on Craigslist.

Most any item has the potential to sell as long as the price is right. Walk through your house, garage, shed, etc. and look for items that you think you can sell.

You can also scout stores for items to resell. You will want items that you can reasonably sell for at least three times what you pay for them, so don't grab anything at the dollar store unless you think people would find it a great deal for $3 or more. It's also worth a swing past the clearance racks at your favorites stores. I generally only purchase things that I think are cute and that are at least 80% off the original price. That means I can ask 60% of the retail price and still get several times my investment back. Anything less is generally not worth the trouble.

If you can wait for inbound cash for at least a week, eBay (http://www.ebay.com) is also a good option. Set up 3-day auctions, and you will usually be able to get the funds back to your bank account within the week for items that sell.

Personal Services:

By "personal services", I mean things you do for an individual (not a company) where they would reasonably expect to pay you on the spot.

Here are a few ideas to get you started:

- Housecleaning: not much fun, but I find you can charge $20/hour or more in most places and collect payment immediately. Advertise your services on craigslist (http://www.craigslist.org), and hopefully you will pick up a couple of jobs in the short term.

- Childcare: Offering emergency or on-call childcare can be a way to bring in some additional income quickly. You can offer overnight or sick child services at your home if you have children to watch.

- Yard work: many people are looking for someone to help take care of their yard and you can likely pick up some quick extra work with a posting to rake leaves, shovel snow, weed flowerbeds or trim hedges. It is not easy work, but it is immediate cash.

- Other services that you are skilled in, like alterations, house painting, or potty training. Post an ad on craigslist.org (http://www.craigslist.org) to see if you can find some quick interest in your skills.

- Planned business offering. You may be able to kill two birds with one stone by offering your new services for half price or some other discount to the first couple of customers with the agreement that they are reference customers for you and will provide a quote on your services that you can include in your marketing. This can get you some quick cash, a couple of great quotes for your prospective new clients, and some potential long-term clients (make the discount for a set period of time).

On any personal services, negotiate the details of the service you'll provide first. It's quite reasonable to let them know you need cash payment the first time since you haven't worked with them before. That makes sure you have cash in your hand when you leave!

Other Ideas:

Bring in a roommate. If you have a bedroom you can free up in your home, you can bring in a roommate. A college student might be appropriate if you are hoping this isn't a long term solution, as they will likely just need housing for the remainder of the school year or the length of the summer break. It would be usual to charge them up front for their rent and for them to pay monthly. You can also ask for a deposit but don't spend it, as you are legally required to return it unless it has to be used to repair damage or clean their space. To increase your income from this you can include "board", which means that you cook enough for them also at mealtimes. They would also need a key to your home, a location to park their car (on the street is OK), access to your laundry machines, space in the refrigerator, etc.

Don't do this if you will be uncomfortable with someone in your space, and pick carefully. It would be good to check references before you allow someone access to your home unsupervised.

One advantage to having a roommate is you may be able to arrange childcare with them, which would allow you some additional time to work or perhaps the ability to work outside your home and generate some additional income.

Take out a loan: Of course, the danger of this is that a loan needs paid back! If you pledge your car or personal items as collateral for a title loan or at a pawn shop, you may lose them if you can't pay back the loan. If you borrow from a friend, you are basically pledging your friendship - and you'll lose it if you don't keep your promise on repayment (and maybe more as well, if they tell others that you didn't keep your word).

Take a job that includes tips. If you have a background in bartending or waitressing, you may be able to find a position right away. The paycheck will take a while to show, but if you take great care of your customers, you will be able to pocket some cash tips right away.

Perform for cash. If your skills include singing, dancing, or musical ability you may want to head to a busy intersection and set up a performance! Hopefully the tips in your hat or guitar case will cover a trip to the grocery store. A similar gig would be looking for jobs to wave signs or dress up in costume to advertise a business or some new homes. These often pay in cash.

Chapter Summary

I hope you'll never need it, but if you are having a cash lull and need some funds urgently, look for opportunities to:

- Sell items in person, such as a garage sale or a posting on craigslist (http://www.craigslist.org).

- Perform personal services, such as housecleaning, yard work or childcare where you can reasonably expect to be paid cash at the time of service.

Designing Your Business

6

Business Services

Businesses, especially small ones, tend to outsource a number of different services since they won't have the need for a full time employee with expertise in that particular area. They are also often very flexible about where the work is performed, which gives you the opportunity to set it up to work exclusively out of your home if you wish to.

These are the big issues you need to address to build a business providing outsourced services to business customers:
1. What services will you offer?
2. How much will you charge?
3. How will you get your information to prospective customers so they can hire you?
4. How will you manage your projects, billings, etc. so that you are paid for the work you do and so you have reference customers going forward?

The different services that businesses purchase are pretty much limitless, though you may have a higher chance of getting several customers up front if you are in the range of services often purchased from an offsite independent contractor.

Here's a quick list of common ones to get you started:

- Website design: this is the creation or update of a website. You don't necessarily need to know CGI and HTML. Many sites are now being created using WordPress templates, which requires much less technical knowledge. If you are good at things like this, check out a book from the library or look for online tutorials to get you started, and set up your first site for yourself! WordPress (http://wordpress.com/) offers free hosting for a basic site and blog.

- Graphic design: this is the creation of graphic elements, such as headers and buttons for websites, covers for books, and logos, marketing brochures and stationary items for businesses.

- Marketing consultant: this is the development of marketing materials for a business, such as brochures and websites (or coordination of the development effort if this is a larger project with all the pieces subcontracted out), and/or development of a plan to reach prospective customers with information about the business to increase sales.

- Research online or via phone: this could include researching specific topics for an author working on a book, locating the names of companies in specific fields or locations for marketing efforts, or contacting clients of a business or specific positions in multiple companies to ask survey questions.

- Lead generation: this is contacting specific types of businesses or individuals and reading a sales script to them, then passing on any initial interest to the company so they can follow up with sales information.

- Marketing writer: this is writing copy for marketing materials to increase the company's sales.

- Technical writer: this is taking documents, in particular descriptions on how to use software or other more technical issues, and re-writing them so that the users of the software will be able to understand and use them.

- Editor: this is reviewing previously written work for errors in spelling or grammar or more broadly for errors or potential improvements in a document or story.

- Translator: this is taking previously written work and re-writing it in a different language.

- Virtual assistant: this is performing various administrative tasks, such as writing memos or letters, reviewing and sorting mail, answering inquiries with basic information, setting up appointments or reservations, and tracking progress on projects via online methods (as opposed to sitting in their office).

- Bookkeeper: this is taking financial information of the business, including bills, checks written, customer invoices, customer payments, and banking information and entering it into a tracking system or accounting software system. It would generally include reconciling to the bank statement, and providing regular (usually monthly) income and expense information.

If you have a technical background, there are many technical jobs available as well. Those fields tend to use offsite contractors at a higher rate than many others and there are a lot of part time telecommute positions available.

In addition, there are lots more business services out there. To get more ideas, do some browsing of contractors and positions on Elance (http://www.elance.com).

Getting Customers

Local Marketing:

Here are ways to locate customers when you provide your services in person and need local people to know about them:

Find a Referrer

Once you've defined something that you're good at and willing to do, you need to find an interested market for those services. One of the best ways to do this is by locating referrers. This will be groups or individuals that have a high need for your services or that work with people that do.

For example, I offer bookkeeping and payroll services. When I relocated, I contacted a number of CPAs in my area with the idea that they are already in contact with many businesses that might need my services. After many contacts, I did find one who had clients needing these services and didn't want to offer them himself, but was looking for someone to assist him. I've been doing bookkeeping for several of his clients for many years at this point. He even drops their information by my house once he obtains it from them each month. I then send their financial statements to him via email, and he forwards them on to his clients with a letter.

Once you start thinking along these lines, you will find many ideas of potential referrers. For instance, do you teach piano lessons? How about checking with local piano stores and see if they offer new customers a list of people teaching lessons? Or, see if local mothers groups and twins clubs have a resource list where you can list your night nanny or meal prep services?

Attend a Business Meet-Up

At Meetup.com, you can search for local business get-togethers. At the time of this writing, there is a link on the left for "Career and Business" that lists many different options. If one of them sounds compatible, go and check it out! Be sure and take along some cards or flyers to hand out to any prospective customers or referrers.

Become an Expert

One good way to meet prospective customers is to get a speaking gig on a topic that your customers might find interesting. Being the speaker makes you an expert in the field - just the type of person they would need to solve their problem!

You can locate speaking opportunities by contacting various organizations in your area, including the Chamber of Commerce and local organizations that might be interested in your expertise. For example, talk to the local American Marketing Association group if your presentation is on marketing.

Post on Local Websites, Such as Craigslist

Many people look on Craigslist (http://www.craigslist.org) for service providers when they don't have a referral from a friend or business acquaintance. For example, I've personally hired bookkeepers, yard work help, babysitters and nannies, and tutors through the site. It's free to post your service, so write up a description of the services you offer and re-post it as it ages off their site.

I've also found a website called Thumbtack (http://www.thumbtack.com) that allows you to post a profile and then use it to automatically post a nicely formatted ad to craigslist regularly - a real time-saver and free to use.

Post at Businesses Where Your Prospective Customers Shop

The premier example of this is putting a flyer up at the grocery store! Many small businesses will have an area where you can leave a card or flyer as well.

Join a Formal Networking Group

There are many formal networking groups out there where members try to come each week with a referral or two for other group members. Two of the best known are BNI and LeTip. There are fees to join and you have to be available for the meeting each week, but if you are able to make that work, you might find these groups to be very beneficial. Even if you aren't able to join a formal group, you can generally audit (visit) a group for free, so you might arrange for childcare and make the rounds of each group in your area to meet the members and let them know about your services. Contact the groups before you show up. Some will only let visitors attend on a formal visitors' day. It's also best to visit a number of groups before you select one to join, so this type of process is a good one if you are planning to join a group as well. Be prepared with a pile of business cards or flyers to take advantage of this opportunity.

There are many professional organizations that meet monthly. You could attend at least once to see if they are a good fit for your business and to pass out some cards or flyers. Examples include: AMA (American Marketing Association), NAWBO (National Association of Women Business Owners), ABWA (American Business Women's Association), and local Chamber of Commerce mixers. In my area (a fairly small town), there are three women's business organizations with meetings at least monthly, two chambers of commerce, a monthly breakfast networking event that attracts hundreds of people, and many different industry or professional meetings, so you can definitely find groups in your area to check out as well. If you're not sure what's available, try asking your local chamber if they have a list of local networking and industry groups, and also try an online search on "business networking XXX" where XXX is your city and state.

If you join a networking group, stay focused on the process of looking for leads for other group members and contacting any leads they give you. Things will often not work in an obvious way, where you receive a lead, call them, and end up with a job. Instead, many will not work out, and others will work out in unexpected ways. For example, I have been working with a company for the past 10 years that sent a representative as a guest to a networking group I belonged to. He never joined, but he did get my card before he left the meeting. Later the company owner got in touch, and we've been working together on various projects ever since. I also asked once at a networking meeting for leads on a non-profit I could volunteer with, since I wasn't very busy and thought it would give me some new skills and get me out of the house! A gal in the group said she had a friend whose husband ran a non-profit that might be able to use my help. Several calls later, I ended up meeting with him, and he told me at that meeting that he didn't want me as a volunteer, instead he'd like to hire me. I've been with them for 11 years at this writing, and they have referred me to several other non-profits as well.

Share Your Information With Other Organizations

Post a description of your services at other websites that might include interested buyers. For example, your photography services and classes might be of interest to mom groups, homeschool lists, and marketing networking groups. You might even offer a special price or discount to anyone they refer you to that mentions the group, to encourage them to pass your information on if they run into a friend who is looking for services like yours.

Online Marketing:

Here are ways to market your services online, if the work is done at your location and delivered electronically to the customer:

Become an Expert - Online

In my experience, this is a longer path to gaining customers than some of the others but don't rule it out, especially if you are a good writer. To become an online expert you would generally:

- Develop a blog or website with outstanding content in the area you provide consulting in. If you offer website marketing services, you would write articles on search engine optimization, where to market your website, how to increase the number of visitors, etc.

- Bring customers to your site through guest blog posts on other sites and through posting outstanding articles on article database websites with your website in the resource box. (If you aren't familiar with them, these are places that writers can post articles they've written with a resource box at the end that includes a brief blurb about the author and a website or other link the reader can go to for more information. Then, websites or bloggers can post these articles for free on their site or blog as long as the resource page linking back to the author is included. If you do this, be sure and make your resource box link compelling, like "Joe Black is an expert on quick easy ways to increase traffic to your web site. Click on the link below for a free eBook on the very best website marketing techniques".) The largest of these are hubpages.com, ezinearticles.com and ideamarketers.com.

- Offer a free book or top 10 list for download for visitors that sign up for your email or blog list.

- Send out high interest articles regularly (most guides say at least weekly) with a clickable link to information about your consulting services.

Market Your Services at Elance

At this writing, ELance (http://www.elance.com) is the largest website to connect freelancers with hirers. The economics depends on your hourly rate and the number of jobs you win. Keep in mind that you don't necessarily have to have the lowest price to win projects. For example, I hired a US consultant when I wanted my website updated, because I was concerned about communication issues with the (much less expensive) overseas contractors. You can also differentiate yourself based on your background and experience to make yourself an obvious choice due to your specialized expertise. I've hired translators via Elance, and definitely had a preference for those who'd previously done similar projects.

To get started, go to Elance and set up an account. During the setup process, you will describe the skills you have to offer prospective clients. You may also have the opportunity to take various tests to prove your skill in different areas.

Once your account is set up, you can search the available jobs and find jobs to bid on. In your bid, you will have room to describe your qualifications and how they relate to the position.

You can bid a fixed or hourly price for the task and propose a delivery date.

Selling services on Elance works well with kids since you can work on the project any time of the day or night you find you have available time; just make sure to meet your delivery dates so your customer reviews will be favorable. These good reviews will then help you get additional business in the future.

I'd also recommend you set up some standard searches right away and have them notify you whenever new projects are posted that meet your requirements since the first bidders on any project have an advantage.

To market on Elance, you probably need the following:

- Some sort of skill that is easy to sell online. Elance has a wide variety of services available, from technical skills to writing to translating.

- Good organizational skills, to make sure you keep in touch with customers during projects to keep them happy and to make sure you regularly check Elance for new opportunities. The first bidders on a project have the highest chance of winning it, since a prospective buyer may tire after reviewing multiple submissions. In addition, I've found I've never hired anyone who wouldn't send in a bid the first time around. It just wasn't worth it to me to have a lengthy discussion with that person when I had many other good looking offers with pricing attached.

To improve your earnings once you're established, you could:

- Offer additional services on the site

- Raise your rates

- Keep in touch with prior customers to see if they have additional needs

Market at Other Freelance Sites Online

Elance is the largest of the freelance job sites, but certainly not the only one. Here are some other similar sites worth looking into:

- Guru http://www.guru.com

- oDesk http://www.odesk.com

- Sologig http://www.sologig.com

- iFreelance http://www.ifreelance.com

- GoFreelance http://www.gofreelance.com

- Freelancer http://www.freelancer.com

- PeoplePerHour http://www.peopleperhour.com

- Monster http://www.monster.com - primarily traditional jobs, but there are some contract and freelance positions posted

- Craigslist http://www.craigslist.org

- Dice http://www. dice.com - mostly technical positions

- Fiverr http://www.fiverr.com - you post things you're willing to do for $5 here, and people can hire you to do them.

7

Personal Services

Personal services is just that... helping someone else with something they either aren't skilled at or don't have time or ability to do themselves. Many of these services have the advantage that they are recurring, meaning that once you are hired, you'll come back on a regular basis so you won't need to continually find new customers. Sometimes you will need to be available at a time set by the customer, but often these services can be performed at your convenience within some parameters, such as while they're at work or as long as you deliver the finished item by Friday. It's also appropriate for most personal services to receive payment at the time the services are delivered or in advance. For example, if you provide dog-walking services, you would likely arrange either to pick up payment each time you walk the dog, or to receive payment monthly on the first for the month ahead.

Here are a few things to think about before you take that first client:

When You're Available

Be realistic about how many hours you have available and things that might prevent you from showing up. Once customers start to count on your services to make their lives easier, they will be annoyed if you don't come. After a couple of misses, they are likely to hire someone else! If you are available while your kids are in school but can't ever come on school holidays, make sure you know when those days are and cover this up front with your customers - perhaps you'll do an extra visit right before the holiday break, or don't work on Wednesdays because school is only a half day.

How to Price Your Services

Your first step in pricing is to determine the usual pricing for that service in your area. You can look online at local companies or people offering those services, contact friends who may use those services to find out what they are paying, or contact other providers and ask them directly.

Once you know the usual range in your area, you can decide on your pricing strategy. Options include pricing your services at a market average, or higher than average (to show quality or reflect specialty skills) or lower than average (to try to bring in more customers right away).

Methods of Payment

It's best to discuss payment with customers right up front, before you complete your work and they look at you with a blank expression on their face. :) Be sure to tell them the amount you are charging them for the services, when you anticipate being paid (as soon as you're done with the work? Monthly in advance?), and what type of payments you accept (cash only? Checks OK? First visit cash required?)

How to Find Customers

And now the biggest one of all - how do you locate people who might need your services?

You should pursue three avenues for finding customers for your services business. These are all appropriate for a small business you are pursuing part time. If your goal is to build a large plumbing agency with multiple employees, you would probably want to include a Yellow Pages ad in your program, and perhaps coupons in the newspaper or the coupon books sent out in most cities. However, as an independent businessperson working part time with no staff, you'll need to be frugal and efficient with your marketing efforts.

Here are the three avenues I'd recommend:

1. Personal referrals: this is when someone tells a friend who's looking for services like yours about you. To build this, you will want to make sure your friends know about the services you now offer. Send out an email to your friends, post on your Facebook page, post on the forum at any organizations you belong to, hand out business cards or flyers at meetings or events - not so that your friends can hire you (although they might!), but so they know what you have to offer. Then when one of their friends asks them if they know anyone who walks dogs, makes dresses, handles bookkeeping, has a mornings-only preschool, etc., they think to recommend you! You might also hand out cards for a discount or referral bonus to your existing customers that they can give to a friend who needs your services.

2. Word of Mouth: this is when you make an arrangement with a person or business to refer you.

For example, there's an organization called The International Organization of the Rainbow for Girls - it's the girls division of the Masons. The girls (aged 11 to 20) in this organization dress very formally and generally need a new floor length formal dress about twice per year. Many of these dresses have to be made since they require a specific fabric for a specific event. If you are an excellent seamstress and able to make dresses, you could get in contact with one of the Rainbow Girls groups through their Mother Advisor, the adult who is currently running the group. In my area, there are several groups and contact information is available on the internet. Once you get in touch with the Mother Advisor, you can let them know your expertise and perhaps even offer to make a simple item or do some alterations for them for free to display your skill. Once they gain confidence in your abilities, they can pass your contact information on to their group and you then have the potential of making quite a large quantity of dresses for this group each year.

There are many similar situations you might be able to come up with. Karate students need their patches transferred to their new uniforms when they outgrow a current one or earn a level requiring a new color of uniform. If you can sew on those patches accurately, leave a card at the desk that they can pass on to students when they pick up new uniforms. People who purchase pianos may need lessons, so see if the local piano stores will pass on your information to people who want piano lessons in their home for their children (or whatever your specific business model is, perhaps it's group lessons at your house instead). People with new babies may need a lot of extra help. Post information about your night nanny service, or meal prep assistance, or house cleaning business with local moms groups, and leave some small stuffed toys for new moms with your church or a nanny service to hand out for new babies with a tag showing your services and contact info.

3. Online or flyer advertising: Many people looking for service providers now look in the Services section of craigslist (http://www.craigslist.org). It's free to post your information, so why not have an advertisement of your services out there? A similar option is to post a flyer on the bulletin board in local grocery stores. Include tear-off pieces at the bottom with your contact information. These are both inexpensive and only take a few minutes to implement.

Personal Service Business Ideas

Here are some potential personal service businesses you could offer. Implement as is, or use them to get your ideas flowing and come up with your own unique business.

Errands and Shopping

What Is It?

Taking care of errands or doing shopping for those who are too busy or are unable to go themselves. Perhaps they are ill, just had surgery, or have a new baby in the house.

Economics

Generally, this is an hourly service. In my area, $20 an hour seems to be common. There might be an additional gas charge if it involves a lot of distance or driving to complete the errands. In addition, any costs incurred are reimbursed.

To Improve Your Earnings

Get several customers who need similar errands done so you can make a single stop and take care of multiple customers.

Necessary Skills

To make this job work you probably need the following:

- Good organizational skills to make sure you take care of all needed errands and to keep careful track of receipts and costs incurred.

What You Need to Get Started

Reliable transportation would be the primary need. In addition, you might need some cash available to purchase items that the customer would reimburse you for.

Making it Work With Kids

You should generally be able to take children along with you in this business as long as they are able to ride in the car and help you with the errands without difficulty.

Pre-Prep Meals

What Is It?

Preparing ingredients so your customers can quickly cook tasty meals on their own.

There are many options you could consider:

- Preparing meals that are frozen and then reheated.

- Preparing ingredients for meals that are frozen. The customer thaws them out and cooks according to the directions you put on the package.

- Preparing dry mixes, either for quick baking or in pretty jars for gifts.

- Preparing "new home" baskets for realtors or apartment managers to give to new residents. For example, spaghetti, a jar of sauce, parmesan cheese, dry breadsticks, and Italian cookies would not need refrigeration and would keep for quite a while. Attach a small label with directions and a place for the giver to attach a business card.

- Preparing "quick meal" baskets for gifts to new parents or college students.

Economics

This can vary widely, depending on what sort of services you provide. I'd suggest contacting other businesses that offer items similar to your product or service to get an idea of competitor pricing. Once you have pricing, keep careful track of your time and costs to make sure you're being fairly compensated for your work.

To Improve Your Earnings

- Increase the types of products you offer

- Locate additional types of businesses or individuals who might need your products.

Necessary Skills

To make this job work, you probably need the following:

- Good organizational skills to keep track of time, costs, and delivery dates for your items.

What You Need to Get Started

- Some samples - either sample menus for the pre-prep meals or sample products for the baskets.

- You may need some sort of health department certification or license to offer these services. Contact your local health department and explain the types of items you will be selling to find out the rules in your area.

- To prepare pre-prep meals, you might need access to a commercial kitchen. If this is the case, call around to various organizations that might not need their kitchen at all times, such as cooking schools that only teach at night, community colleges that don't always have students, or similar businesses that will let you lease a station for a few hours a week.

Making it Work With Kids

In general, this business would involve doing work at your home plus running around to purchase materials and deliver finished items. As long as your children are able to go shopping and ride in the car with you, you can probably just bring them along. You may even be able to allow them to help you when doing the production work at home.

Catering or Home Chef

What Is It?

Preparing food for parties or events, or for a family to eat at home.

Economics

Generally, this type of work pays a fixed price per person or meal. Catering might be $20 per person for a specific menu selection and meals prepared for a family might be $30 for a serving for four. You'll need to describe exactly what's included in terms of sides, desserts, etc.

To figure out your profit, you'll need to keep close track of your time and expenses to make sure you're getting fair compensation for your efforts.

To Improve Your Earnings

- Increase the number of meals prepared at the same time for economies of scale (meaning you can chop vegetables for 10 meals in about twice the time as vegetables for one meal since the setup time is about the same).

- Increase your purchase quantities as you have more meals to prepare to reduce your ingredient prices.

- Shop sales and design meal options around your purchases.

Necessary Skills

To make this job work, you probably need the following:

- Excellent cooking skills

- A background in preparing large amounts of food is helpful if you will be catering

What You Need to Get Started

A location to prepare the food. If you are a home chef, you can likely use the client's kitchen and will just need to bring the appropriate food with you to prepare. If you are catering for a large event, you may need access to a commercial kitchen; contact different locations that have one to see if they will let you rent the space during their off hours. You'll also need appropriate transportation and serving equipment if you are catering parties to keep the food at a safe temperature prior to serving.

Making it Work With Kids

It's probably helpful to have someone else to watch your children while you prepare food for a big party or event since the interruptions could impact your quality. There also may be rules that you need to comply with regarding outside people in the kitchen area while food is prepared for sale. You'll need a sitter when serving food at the event, unless your children are old enough to help.

House Cleaning

What Is It?

Cleaning houses for homeowners who don't have time, for realtors if the home is for sale, or for apartment or rental house owners upon tenant move-out.

Economics

Generally, this type of work is done on an hourly basis. In my area, people will come and look at the premises and provide a flat quote. I've found that the quotes work out to about $20 per hour. You'll want to specify up front whether you will supply the cleaning supplies and equipment (such as a vacuum) or if the owner will provide.

To Improve Your Earnings

- Provide more specialized cleaning services, such as pet smell removal or full house spring cleaning (with windows and baseboards).

- You may be able to offer minor repair work if you are able to do it, such as touch up painting or re-gluing loose tiles, for a higher hourly rate while you are onsite.

Necessary Skills

To make this job work, you probably need the following:

- Good attention to detail to make sure you leave the home looking clean.

- Reliable transportation and willingness to show up when expected. Once people get used to having this service, they will hire someone else if you don't come when expected.

What You Need to Get Started

- It would be a good idea to be bonded, as many people will not be comfortable with you in their home if you are not. Contact your insurance company for information on this.

- You will need cleaning supplies unless the owner is providing.

Making it Work with Kids

Since you will be in someone else's home or property, you should probably leave the kids at home. This would be a business where you need a spouse, friend or sitter to watch your children while you work.

Landscaping or Yard Work

What Is It?

Determining the arrangement of new plants and other materials in a yard, taking care of existing plants by weeding or trimming, or providing seasonal yard work such as raking leaves and preparing flowerbeds.

Economics

Landscaping design work requires a license in some states, so you'll want to check your local requirements before taking on any large or commercial jobs.

Developing a small plan for a local homeowner is OK in most places as long as you don't present yourself as a professional landscape designer.

Generally, design work is done for a flat rate quoted to the customer, and utilizes landscape software to show how the final design will look in different seasons as well as after several years of growth.

Changing out plants or installing sod, maintenance work like mowing and weeding, and seasonal work like raking leaves is often hourly work at a rate of $10 to $25 an hour. If you are good at estimating your time to do a job, calculate it at the higher rate and offer a flat rate to complete the work. For example, say, "I'd charge $50 to rake and bag all those leaves". If you can do it in two hours, you've earned $25 an hour.

You can also often negotiate a flat rate for maintenance work, especially if you provide any tools needed. In my area, a lawn mow and edge for an average yard is $25 and takes less than 30 minutes, so if the customers are close together you could do two jobs in an hour.

To Improve Your Earnings

Flat rates are often the way to go, as people may balk at a higher hourly rate but are OK with a flat rate that seems appropriate to them. Make sure you are good at defining exactly what work will be completed, and at determining the time you'll need to complete that work.

Necessary Skills

To make this job work, you probably need the following:

- You'll need to be in good physical shape for this type of work

- You'll need the ability to operate common yard work tools such as lawn mowers and hedge trimmers

What You Need to Get Started

You can get started just by getting your first customer, but you can charge higher and flat rates if you have your own equipment. You'll need basic equipment such as a lawn mower, hedge trimmer, edger, and leaf rake, plus a way to transport them (i.e., a pickup or trailer). You can purchase these items at garage sales if you don't have a lot of cash to start.

Making it Work with Kids

Since you are outside, your kids can generally come along as long as they stay out of the way of any equipment. However, it's best not to let them help unless they are old enough to get a good amount of work done and unless you let the client know in advance. If you have quoted a flat rate, there will usually not be an objection. If you're working for an hourly rate, you'll either need to include their work for free or explain up front that you'll have a "helper" and what their rate will be. A middle school helper might be at a lower rate, whereas a high school-age son might be full rate since they are able to accomplish as much as an adult.

Personal Assistant

What Is It?

A personal assistant assists someone with administrative tasks and errands, as needed. It may include tasks such as picking up mail, typing letters, making phone calls and appointments, and delivering completed work to clients or an office.

Economics

Generally, this type of work is done on an hourly basis. Depending on your skills, it would likely vary between $10 and $40 per hour.

To Improve Your Earnings

- Offer specialized skills, such as spreadsheet or database work.

- Hire an assistant to help with easier routine work at a lower hourly rate than you are charging the client. You are still responsible for the quality of their work, so you'll need to be careful during your hiring process.

Necessary Skills

To make this job work, you probably need the following:

- Skills as needed to perform the work. This will vary quite a bit with different positions.

- Great organizational skills and attention to detail to make sure everything is done to the client's specifications.

What You Need to Get Started

Just a client who needs skills that you already possess.

Making it Work with Kids

Often, this type of work is performed offsite - generally at your home, or while driving in the car, so your children can probably come along with you for most of these positions.

Interior Designer

What Is It?

Providing decorating services for a home or business, including painting, hanging curtains, and selection of furniture and artwork.

Economics

This work can be performed on an hourly or a fixed price basis (you provide a flat dollar price to perform specific services). The specific rates vary widely based on your experience and the customer's needs, so you'll want to do some research locally to determine your prices. In addition, designers normally charge a percentage markup (about 10%) on all items selected for purchase, such as artwork and furniture.

To Improve Your Earnings

- Once you have some happy clients to refer you and talk to prospective clients about your work, you can likely raise your rates.

Necessary Skills

To make this job work, you probably need the following:

- The ability to listen to your client's goals and translate them into appropriate design and furniture decisions.

- It would likely be helpful to have some basic installation skills so you don't have to outsource all the work.

What You Need to Get Started

Just that first client. Start by announcing your new business to friends and family to see if you can get a "friendly" as your first customer.

Making it Work with Kids

When you are at someone else's home or property, you should probably leave the kids at home with a spouse, friend or sitter. They can come along when you are shopping for furniture and materials as long as they are able to be patient while you shop.

Seamstress

What Is It?

Making custom clothing for people, altering existing clothing for people, or sewing household items to order, such as curtains and slipcovers, or sewing custom items to order or to sell.

Economics

The economics will depend on your specific offerings. In general, flat rates are quoted for specific work, so you'll need to keep close track of your hours and materials to make sure you're charging a fair rate for your efforts.

To Improve Your Earnings

If you make custom items, you may also want to sell them online. I have purchased handmade tote bags, crib sets, and portable crib sheets on ebay.com. If you have the skills to make items like these, put together some nice items or sets and sell them online on eBay or Etsy (lots more about this in the "Sell Products Online" chapter).

Necessary Skills

To make this job work, you probably need the following:

- Excellent sewing skills.

- Good organizational skills to make sure work is ready on time and to track all your time and expenses to make sure you're making money from your venture.

What You Need to Get Started

In general, you'll just need a sewing machine and a selection of basic supplies like thread and pins. The features of the machine will determine what you can offer. For example, you'll need an embroidery machine to embroider names on karate uniforms. If you're going to make custom items, you'll also need a stock of fabric. Be creative if you need to. A bed sheet in good condition can be converted into custom clothing items or crib sheets, and used but very good condition sheets are much less expensive to purchase (think garage sales!) than new fabric. (Some of you are thinking "gross!" about now, but really...just wash it, it will be OK! Plus you're helping the environment by reusing items that might otherwise be thrown away.)

You will also want to start making contacts who can send customers to you. For example, I talked earlier about the International Order of the Rainbow for Girls. Girls in this organization need an average of two long dresses made for them each year, so a contact at that organization could bring in a lot of work. Many small clothing shops and dry cleaners outsource alterations work, and a local furniture store might be happy to have a name of someone who can make curtains to match a customer's new furniture purchase.

Making it Work with Kids

Since most of this work will be done at your home, it's easy to combine with children. You can have people come to your location for fittings as well.

Fitness Instructor or Personal Trainer

What Is It?

Leading group fitness classes or helping individuals set up and maintain an exercise program.

Economics

This can vary widely, depending greatly on whether you work for an existing program where they locate customers and pay you a fee, or whether you design and set up your own program and locate your own customers. For example, in my area, it would be usual to pay $40 to $50 per hour for a personal trainer. If you locate the customer yourself and work with them, those funds are yours. However, if you work for a gym that locates the customer and schedules them with you, you will likely get only $10 to $20 for that hour of your time. Group classes are a similar situation. If you work for an organization and teach the fitness class, they will likely pay you an hourly fee, or in some cases a set amount per student who attends. However, if you locate the customers yourself for your Boot Camp or Step Aerobics course, the fees will all come to you.

There is a complication to setting classes up yourself - in addition to the marketing effort, you need to find a place to hold the course. A Boot Camp might be easy - have everyone meet you at a park, for example. For personal training, you need a location with the appropriate equipment and that will allow you to bring in clients and work with them (gyms that offer their own personal training often don't allow this).

To Improve Your Earnings

- Offer or teach additional courses

- If you are paid per attendee, teach larger groups

- Offer specialized courses, which you can charge a higher fee for - perhaps "post-baby" classes, sports skills courses for specific sports, or courses using specialized exercises like Pilates.

- Raise your rates once you have several clients who are willing to be references and a mostly full schedule. It is probably better not to do this too soon since you may lose a few customers and bring on fewer new ones, but if you have the skills and expertise, you should definitely be paid appropriately.

Necessary Skills

To make this job work, you probably need the following:

- A high level of fitness. It often takes more energy to teach the course than attend it since you will have to speak while demonstrating. If you are a personal trainer, your own physique is your best advertisement, so you'll want it to be at least "better than average".

- A fitness certification of some sort, both so that you have the appropriate training and knowledge to avoid hurting your clients, and so that you can obtain insurance in case someone does get hurt. There are a number of different certification programs out there. The ones that appear to have the most credibility are ACE, NSCA, ISSA and ACSM. Research before you select your certification. Contact fitness programs and ask them the type of certification their trainers or instructors have. There are also many online "certifications" that will send you a certificate for a nominal fee and a short questionnaire but that won't actually give you any marketable skills or training, so beware of scams!

What You Need to Get Started

In general, just a job as a fitness instructor or a client and a place to teach them. As discussed above, certification is also a good idea, though not always a necessary step.

Making it Work with Kids

In some cases, this is easy - if you're teaching a Baby Bootcamp class and have a baby, bring them along! Many fitness centers will have a childcare center and allow their instructors to leave their children there free of charge while they are teaching a course at the center.

In the case of other fitness courses or one-on-one personal training, you will likely need to make childcare arrangements with a spouse, friend or sitter.

8

Teaching

If you enjoy teaching others new things, you can likely build a business from it. Parents want their children to have many different experiences and skills and likely won't be able to provide all the training themselves. Many adults are going back to school to improve their skills, so there is a market for teaching or tutoring them as well. Read on for ways to take your love for helping others and turn it into a business.

Tutoring – In Person or Online

What Is It?
Helping kids with homework or other school skills, including reading, math, other academic subjects, study skills, and organizing work.

Economics
In my area, individual tutoring rates vary from about $10 to $30 an hour, depending on the difficulty of the study and the qualifications of the tutor. You could also offer group tutoring in specific subjects or for specific test preparation. The rate would be lower, perhaps $5 to $10 an hour per student, but you could teach several students at once.

To Improve Your Earnings
- Focus on group tutoring. Larger groups can be more profitable, as long as it works with the subject matter

- Raise your rates. You will probably need a few success stories to do so, but once you've dramatically helped those first few children, ask their parents for written testimonials you can share on your website and with prospective clients, and increase your fees.

Necessary Skills
To make this job work, you probably need the following:

- A high level of expertise in the relevant subject area(s)

- Great teaching skills

- Lots of patience and good skills at working with children - especially difficult ones, since the frustration of being behind in school can result in some unpleasant behavior from your clients.

What You Need to Get Started
- Appropriate materials to teach the subjects you offer tutoring in

Making it Work with Kids
Since the parents are paying you to focus on their children's learning needs, it's probably not appropriate to have your children in the same room. You probably need to have a spouse or sitter care for them - in another room if you are tutoring at your home, or somewhere else if you are at a business location or the client's home. Another option is to arrange for a "swap" with another mom who needs time away from her kids as well. You each take a turn with all the children once or twice a week, so the other mom can go to work!

Private Lessons

What Is It?

Teaching private lessons in a field you have a lot of knowledge in. You can modify the options to suit your preferences. For example, language courses can be taught to individuals, families or in a group setting. Piano lessons can be taught at your home or at the client's. Many skills, including foreign languages and technical skills, can be taught online using an online program where the client can see your screen or via video conferencing.

In many areas, there are formal catalogs of courses you can submit a proposal to. Although you will need to give them a percentage or set amount of the proceeds, they will handle marketing (through distributing their catalog of courses), signups and payments, and will often provide or arrange for a room to teach the course in. Once you identify the local providers of these courses, you'll need to evaluate whether your proposed course will fit into their program. If so, call and ask them about the application or proposal process.

In my local area, there are courses through the school district, the community college and the university outreach. In larger cities I've lived in, there were also magazine-type publications that listed lots of courses offered by different people that you could sign up for.

Economics

The economics will vary based on whether you are locating clients yourself or working through a referring organization. You can get a good idea of appropriate rates for locating and teaching clients yourself by looking for other local providers of these services and calling them for their rates and services offered. If you are working through another organization, they will explain their revenue sharing program when you contact them for more information. In my area, lessons such as foreign language and music taught by an experienced instructor to one student run from about $20 - $50 per hour.

To Improve Your Earnings

- Offer additional services that your students may need. You may get some great ideas when contacting other local providers of lessons to determine pricing.

- Raise your hourly rates (if you think your clients will pay it rather than switching to another provider).

- Teach group lessons if it works in your field. You would charge a lower rate to each participant, but require a minimum number of students to sign up to teach the lesson or course, which would result in a higher hourly rate to you.

- Have related products or services available for your clients at a reasonable markup. For example, you could sell music books, language books, uniforms, specialized computer add-on packs such as software, as needed to your students. Please keep in mind that if you are selling goods (as in all of these examples), you will need a sales tax permit from your state tax agency. You'll be able to purchase your goods without paying sales tax (and possibly at a discount), but will need to collect sales tax from your customers and remit it to the state agency on a regular basis, generally monthly or quarterly depending on your sales volume. You'll need to keep careful track of your purchases and sales in this situation. You may also need to provide a security deposit to the taxing agency when setting up your account; in my experience, these are $100 - $200 for a small seller but of course, all agencies will have their own policies.

Necessary Skills

To make this job work, you probably need the following:

- Experience in a field and the ability to teach others your skills. In many fields, you can purchase curriculum if you don't have a lot of experience teaching the skills. This also gives you the opportunity to provide the necessary student materials to your students at a markup.

- Good organizational skills. You will need to track lesson times, billing and payments, student progress so you can make sure the lessons match their current skills and abilities, and probably many other issues relating to your specific offering. It's crucial that you do this well. Even an outstanding teacher will quickly lose students over administrative issues such as missed lessons, and if you aren't good at billing for and collecting payment for lessons, you will quickly find that your students don't pay and will stop coming to see you if you press them. It's an old adage that "the value of services declines after the services are provided". This means that students are much more interested in paying you in advance or immediately upon receipt of the services. As time passes and they forget the benefit they received from your lessons and as their balance creeps up, they will be less and less likely to pay you the amount due.

What You Need to Get Started

The most important thing you need is a plan for the services you will offer and a decision on where and how you will market them.

You should also think through your plan for scheduling and tracking lessons, and invoicing and collecting payments ahead of time. At a minimum, you will need a calendar to track lessons and some way (perhaps even a log) of tracking invoices given to customers and monies collected. There are also online programs available for managing lessons; you may want to look at them to see if it's cost-effective for the size of your business. I did a quick search on Google for "lesson scheduling and invoicing" and came up with several options, including some specifically for tutors and music teachers. These can have additional benefits like sending lessons reminders to your students, allowing for scheduling over the internet, and tracking which bills have been paid.

Making it Work with Kids

Since you're being paid to focus on their learning needs, it's probably not appropriate to have your children in the same room. You probably need to have a spouse or sitter care for them in another room if you are tutoring at your home, or somewhere else if you are at a business location or the client's home. Another option is to arrange for a "swap" with another mom who needs time away from her kids as well - you each take a turn with all the children once or twice a week, so the other mom can go to work!

Teaching Adults

What Is It?

Teaching adults at an educational venue. Most of these will require a master's degree in the subject area you wish to teach, though a trade school might have other requirements showing proficiency in the subject area. You'll also need to show work experience in the field and have good references. Some options for teaching include local community colleges, university extension departments (also called extended studies), trade schools, and the University of Phoenix or other evening adult education programs.

Economics

Compensation for teaching varies. In general, all part time faculty at these institutions will be paid on a comparable basis and you will likely get that information very early in the hiring process. You may even be able to find it online; my local community college states a rate of $730 per credit hour for teaching any of its courses.

To Improve Your Earnings

- Teach additional courses. This includes the obvious benefit of being paid twice as much for two courses, and the fact that some of these institutions provide raises after a certain number of courses are taught.

Necessary Skills

To make this job work, you probably need the following:

- Some natural teaching ability and enjoyment. Many of these venues will offer you formal skills training once you are hired, so you may not need any teaching experience.

What You Need to Get Started

Instructors at these types of programs usually do not need any formal teaching license or experience, but do need a number of years of relevant work experience in a professional related field plus a master's degree in a related field. If you identify potential institutions in your area that might hire part time faculty, you can search online for "(fill in institution name here) employment" and find their employment information page, which will fill you in on the specific requirements at their institution.

Making it Work with Kids

You won't be able to bring your children along, so you'll need assistance from a spouse, friend or sitter.

Teaching Adults Online

What Is It?
Teaching adults in an online forum or classroom. Most of these will require a master's degree in the subject area you wish to teach; some require a doctorate or PhD. You'll also need to show work experience in the field, have good references, and have good computer skills.

Economics
Compensation for teaching varies. In general, all part time faculty at these institutions will be paid on a comparable basis, and you will likely get that information very early in the hiring process. You may even be able to find it online; my local community college states a rate of $730 per credit hour for teaching any of its courses.

To Improve Your Earnings
- Teach additional courses. This includes the obvious benefit of being paid twice as much for two courses, and the fact that some of these institutions provide raises after a certain number of courses are taught.

Necessary Skills
To make this job work, you probably need the following:

- Strong computer skills and a comfort level for sitting at a computer for longer periods of time.

- Good organizational skills to keep up with grading of assignments, online discussions, and other deadlines.

- Reliable high-speed internet at your home and a computer that meets the college's specifications.

What You Need to Get Started

Generally, instructors at these types of programs do not need any formal teaching license or experience, but do need a number of years of relevant work experience in a professional related field plus a master's degree in a related field. Some also require prior online teaching experience.

You can locate the names of the largest online educators on the internet by searching for "largest online universities". Here is an example. These are the seven largest online universities per the Huffington Post as of December 2011(http://www.huffingtonpost.com/2011/12/16/the-7-largest-online-univ_n_1154135.html). It includes:

- University of Phoenix

- Kaplan University

- Strayer University

- Ashford University

- Liberty University

- Walden University

- University of Maryland

These, of course, are only the largest! You can find many more by searching for "largest online university" lists, or by searching for positions in a search engine using "online faculty positions" or a similar search string.

Once you have some names, search online for "(fill in institution name here) employment" and find their employment information page, which will fill you in on the specific requirements at their institution.

You may also find that many local colleges offer some courses online. My local community college has a number of online courses, for example.

There are also some large job sites which include online faculty positions, and that have "job agents" that will send you positions matching a search string every day. I have three different searches I use for online positions: "online faculty", "online instructor" and "faculty - online". These are the sites I've found to have quite a few positions listed:

- Simply Hired http://www.simplyhired.com

- Higher Ed Jobs http://www.higheredjobs.com

- Indeed http://www.indeed.com

Making it Work with Kids
Since you are working from your home, you'll just need some uninterrupted time to work. In most of the institutions, that can be any time of day as long as it's on a regular schedule. You may need two-hour blocks, four days a week, for example.

Homeschool or After-School Enrichment

What Is It?

Teaching specific courses or skills for either homeschoolers or for after school enrichment. Since these are "enrichment", you won't need a teaching license. It's comparable to providing music or language lessons, but in another enrichment area such as science, mythology, art, or some other subject you have a lot of knowledge and enthusiasm in.

Economics

The economics will vary based on whether you are locating clients yourself or working through a referring organization. You can get a good idea of appropriate rates for locating and teaching clients yourself by looking for other local providers of these services and calling them for their rates and services offered. If you are working through another organization, they will explain their revenue sharing program when you contact them for more information. In my area, I'd anticipate group lessons to run $5 to $10 per student per hour; prices would likely be higher in urban areas and for more specialized subjects.

To Improve Your Earnings

- Increase your class sizes, if appropriate for the subject you teach

- Offer higher-end "specialty" courses at a higher rate

- Have related products or services available for your clients at a reasonable markup. This might include a course materials fee that covers the cost of items needed for the course at a flat rate, for example.

- Experience in a field and the ability to teach others your skills. In many fields, you can purchase curriculum if you don't have a lot of experience teaching the skills. This also gives you the opportunity to provide the necessary student materials to your students at a markup.

- Good organizational skills. You will need to track lesson times, billing and payments, student progress so you can make sure the lessons match their current skills and abilities, and probably many other issues relating to your specific offering. It's crucial that you do this well. Even an outstanding teacher will quickly lose students over administrative issues such as missed lessons, and if you aren't good at billing for and collecting payment for lessons you will quickly find that your students don't pay and will stop coming to see you if you press them. It's an old adage that "the value of services declines after the services are provided". This means that students are much more interested in paying you in advance or immediately upon receipt of the services. As time passes and they forget the benefit they received from your lessons, and as their balance creeps up, they will be less and less likely to pay you the amount due.

What You Need to Get Started

The most important thing you need is a plan for the services you will offer and a decision on where and how you will market them.

You may need to purchase curriculum items.

You should also think through your plan for scheduling and tracking lessons, and invoicing and collecting payments ahead of time. At a minimum, you will need a calendar to track lessons and some way (perhaps even a log) of tracking invoices given to customers and monies collected. There are also online programs available for managing lessons; you may want to look at them to see if it's cost-effective for the size of your business. I did a quick search on Google for "lesson scheduling and invoicing" and came up with several options, including some specifically for tutors and music teachers. These can have additional benefits like sending lessons reminders to your students, allowing for scheduling over the internet, and tracking which bills have been paid.

Making it Work with Kids

If your children are of an appropriate age and it's a group setting, you can probably just include your kids in the group. Otherwise, you probably need to have a spouse or sitter care for them in another room if you are tutoring at your home, or somewhere else if you are at a business location or the client's home. Another option is to arrange for a "swap" with another mom who needs time away from her kids.

9

Childcare

One of the more obvious ways to bring in income when you have children to take care of is to take care of some other children at the same time! Starting a daycare out of your home can be an option, but it's also a big commitment and may limit your flexibility with your own family. In this section, we talk about home daycares, and about other options that can provide income with a bit less commitment.

In-Home Daycare

What Is It?

Traditionally, a daycare is taking care of someone else's child(ren) on an ongoing basis, so perhaps mornings for five days a week, or all day twice a week while they are at work. It can also be full days or even extended 12-hour days or overnight services.

Economics

Pricing of childcare varies widely in different areas, so you will want to do some research on this. One of the easiest ways is to go to craigslist.org and look through the childcare section. You will likely find some posted rates for in-home daycares and if not, you can call a few to find out their hours and pricing.

In my area, $100 to $125 per week for in-home, full-time childcare is a fairly common price point. You also might consider swing shift or overnight care for parents who do shift work, as their might be a lot less competition and your charges will spend a good portion of their time sleeping.

To Improve Your Earnings

- Adjust the number of children you can support, perhaps by hiring an assistant or helper.

- Offer additional services for the children, which you can have provided at your daycare and then mark up or have the vendor provide a percentage back. This might include things like ballet, music lessons, or sports classes.

- Offer meals for a set fee, maybe $2.00 for breakfast and $3.00 for lunch. You can come up with healthy and inexpensive items to serve, such as oatmeal with bananas and milk for breakfast, and beans and rice for lunch.

- Offer extended hours on occasion, such as a "parents' night out", when children stay later so parents can go out to dinner or perhaps on a Saturday day during Christmas shopping season, or be willing to care for children for overnights or weekends away if their parents need to travel.

Necessary Skills

The number one thing you need to make a daycare work is a love for children and the ability to relate well to them. You'll also need to be organized and not sick much, since people will count on you to watch their children while they are at work, and if you aren't available they will have to call in sick and could even lose their job!

What You Need to Get Started

You will need to look into regulations in your area to make sure you're compliant with the law. In many areas, unlicensed childcare is an option as long as you have only a small number of children. You may also need to be licensed (and can charge more if you are licensed), but this adds time, a background check, and the expense of the licensing and inspections. There may be rules you need to comply with in terms of meal preparation (if you offer this).

You'll need an appropriate place to offer care. It will need amenities appropriate for the ages of children you watch, including access to an outside play area, a quiet nap place for younger children, and a place to study for school age kids. You'll need appropriate safety gear in place, especially with younger children, and probably access to a bathroom, kitchen, and washer and dryer. You'll also need an appropriate spot for dirty diapers and other contaminated items, and a way to track different children's bottles, cups, clothes, bags, etc.

It's a good idea to have a special place for messages, perhaps a white board near the phone, so you can document special information such as food allergies, unusual pickup times (so you aren't at the park!), and contact numbers.

Making it Work with Kids

This is one business where it's fairly easy to include your children. You will just need to look into whether they are counted toward any childcare ratios you need to comply with. You'll definitely need to explain to any kids old enough to understand that you'll need to share your time and attention among all the children present.

On-Call or Sick Child Care

What Is It?
Taking care of children who are unable to attend their regular care due to minor illness, or providing emergency childcare for parents who have sudden needs, such as those working for the fire department or on call at the hospital.

Economics
Generally, this would be at an hourly rate, which is higher than the usual childcare in your area due to the on-call nature of it.

To Improve Your Earnings
- Have multiple children at your home during the same time period. For example, it might work if you worked with several families out of the same fire station.

Necessary Skills
For on-call services, you need a fairly flexible schedule so you can be available when needed. If you often aren't, the parents will locate another provider.

For sick child services, in addition to flexibility you will need to be set up for this type of service. Some sort of medical training would be an advantage, especially since children with minor illnesses occasionally become very ill and you'd have the skills to know what to do in that situation.

What You Need to Get Started
You will need to double check regulations in your area before starting a sick child service, as some areas may require medical training to care for children that have illnesses that prevent them from attending their regular care.

Otherwise, you just need a location and license that meet local requirements.

Making it Work with Kids

This is one business where it's fairly easy to include your children; you will just need to look into whether they are counted toward any childcare ratios you need to comply with. You'll definitely need to explain to any kids old enough to understand that you'll need to share your time and attention among all the children present, and help your children understand that they need to leave any sick children alone.

School Holidays/Breaks or After School Care

What Is It?
Offering childcare during school breaks, or offering after-school care where you pick up the children at school and care for them until their parents are off work.

Economics
Pricing of childcare varies widely in different areas, so you will want to do some research on this. One of the easiest ways is to go to craigslist.org and look through the childcare section. You will likely find some posted rates for school break camps and after school care and if not, you can call a few to find out their hours and pricing.

To Improve Your Earnings
- Offer special activities like sports or Spanish. A specialty program will appeal to fewer prospective students, but can be priced higher.

- Offer after school tutoring, or extra lessons such as hands-on science classes or cooking.

Necessary Skills
To make this job work, you probably need the following:

- Great child management skills and an enjoyment of children

- Good organizational skills to make sure the commitments you make to the parents about the type of program or activities their children receive are followed

What You Need to Get Started

You will need to look into regulations in your area to make sure you're compliant with the law. In many areas, unlicensed childcare is an option as long as you have only a small number of children. You may need to be licensed (and can charge more if you are licensed), but this adds time, a background check, and the expense of the licensing and inspections. There may be rules you need to comply with in terms of meal preparation (if you offer this).

You'll need an appropriate place to offer care. It will need amenities appropriate for the ages of children you watch, including access to an outside play area, a quiet nap place for younger children, and a place to study for school age kids. You'll need appropriate safety gear in place, especially with younger children, and probably access to a bathroom, kitchen, and washer and dryer. You'll need an appropriate spot for dirty diapers and other contaminated items, and a way to track different children's bottles, cups, clothes, bags, etc.

It's a good idea to have a special place for messages, perhaps a white board near the phone, so you can document special information such as food allergies, unusual pickup times (so you aren't at the park!), and contact numbers.

Making it Work with Kids

This is one business where it's fairly easy to include your children; you will just need to look into whether they are counted toward any childcare ratios you need to comply with. You'll definitely need to explain to any kids old enough to understand that you'll need to share your time and attention among all the children present.

In-Home Preschool

What Is It?
Children come to your home or location, often for just a few hours a day (I had a friend with a successful preschool that was three afternoons a week) for activities and preschool lessons.

Economics
In general, I see part time programs priced somewhere in the $5 to $10 an hour range, multiplied out to give a flat weekly or monthly rate. Urban areas might be higher. Often, parents sign a contract or pay monthly. No refunds are given, but parents can claim up to a specified amount of vacation time and receive credit for it. In addition, some programs offer discounts for siblings.

If we assume $7 is appropriate in your area and you are offering preschool three mornings a week for three hours, you would charge $7/hour x 3 hours/ day x 3 days/ week x 4 week/month = $252 per month (probably rounded down to $245 or $250, to make it less obvious you are using an hourly rate to calculate it). Using this same logic, the range of $5 to $10 per hour would give a monthly price range of $180 to $360 per month. In my area, I've seen part time programs for five mornings a week priced at $450/month, so the $250/month for three days seems reasonable to me.

The same program I referred to earlier is $550/month for school day (9 - 3:30) and $650/month for extended day (7:30am - 5:30pm). I believe it's common to only add a small fee for the long day service, so in terms of your economics, you may want to stick to just a morning program since it's got the highest effective hourly rate for you. This gives moms a chance to take care of some errands while their children learn, and then take them home for naptime. If you find you need to offer a longer day to get enough customers, you will need to recalculate the hourly rate to make sure it's a worthwhile situation for you as well.

Back to the part time program. If you have five students (probably a good ratio for teaching preschool skills) at $250/month for nine hours weekly of preschool, that works out to an hourly rate of $35. You will probably need some money up front to invest in materials, but most of them will be re-usable, so ongoing costs will be minimal, probably just some snack-time food and consumables like paper and crayons.

To Improve Your Earnings

- Provide a curriculum (or formal learning method) to your students. You can charge a higher rate if you show a formal plan to your prospective parents, and then report back your student's growth against the plan objectives on a regular basis.

Necessary Skills

To make this job work, you probably need the following:

- Love of teaching, and preferably some formal teaching experience as it will improve your credibility with parents

- Love of children and enthusiasm for working with them

What You Need to Get Started

Materials - specifics will vary based on what you plan to teach the children. It will likely include some phonics materials, counters, books, and art supplies. You may be able to get many of these items at garage sales or online at a discount to keep your costs down.

Description of the program - it's a nice touch to have a one page document describing how your run your preschool and what you will be teaching the students. This can include your contact information, and be emailed or handed out to prospective customers.

Making it Work with Kids

As long as your children are not too disruptive, you can just include them! They can join in the lessons if they are of an appropriate age, or play quietly in the room if not. You can also consider offering to keep younger siblings during the lessons for a much lower fee, and hire an assistant who plays games with them in another room along with your children. With a couple of paid siblings, you can likely pay the helper with no cost to you for childcare while you teach your students.

Foster Care

What Is It?

Foster care is having children who, for some reason don't have a home to go to, stay with you rather than at a shelter or center.

Foster care is 24/7, so be sure you're up for it. There are many rules around your care of the children. I believe in my area, it is typical that you need to attend a course before you can apply to accept foster children, and a background check and home study are required as well. There are also rules you'll need to follow in terms of discipline methods and whom you leave the children with. Generally speaking, you cannot leave the children with anyone who is not also certified for foster care, not even one of your older children or a babysitter or relative. You may need to supervise visits of the children with their parents, and may be required to take them to appointments. Some children have additional needs that you would have to manage, such as physical disabilities, medical or therapy appointments, and court dates. You'll have to meet certain requirements in terms of the amount of space in your home. A representative from the foster care system will come regularly to check on the situation. You won't know in advance how long the child will be with you. If the child's parents' rights are terminated, you would generally be allowed to apply to adopt the child permanently. If adopted, payments for foster care would stop.

If you love children and are able to manage the additional rules and requirements, this could be a good option for you. Monthly care payments vary, so you'll need to investigate the local specifics. The payment is higher for special needs children, such as infants or children with disabilities.

Economics

This varies widely in different areas. You can locate information in your area either online by searching for foster care rates in your city and state, or by calling your appropriate local foster care agency.

To Improve Your Earnings

- Offer to care for infants or children with special needs, since the compensation usually increases with the additional needs.

- Offer to house sibling groups, so you would have several related children with you.

Necessary Skills

To make this job work, you probably need the following:

- A love for children

- An ability to handle and work with difficult children, as many foster care children will have unusual circumstances or special needs

- Training, as required by your local foster care agency

What You Need to Get Started

The first step would be to contact your local Child Services agency to get information on program requirements in your area. Usually, you will need to attend an evening class to understand the requirements of the program and make sure you are willing to do it. Then, both a background check and home study are required.

There will be requirements for things like the size of your home and number of bedrooms, which will determine the number of children you are able to care for at any one time. There may be additional needs, such as handicapped access for specific children that might need homes.

Making it Work with Kids

Experienced foster moms tell me that your foster children should always be younger than your biological children are. Sometimes, these children come with behavior or other issues and it is less likely that your children will adopt the behaviors if they are younger.

Night Nanny or New Mom Helper

What Is It?

A new mom helper comes by and helps a new mother by teaching her basic baby care skills and assisting with the child so she can take a walk, take a shower, etc. A night nanny usually comes in the evening after dinner and watches the new baby (or babies,as night nannies are often used by parents of twins) overnight, so the mom can get some much needed rest. In both cases, they will generally help with other things around the house if the baby is sleeping, such as cooking/meal prep, laundry and light housekeeping.

Economics

Generally, night nannies can charge more than their daytime counterparts can. In my area, nannies are usually paid $10 - $13 per hour, but night nannies charge $15 per hour with a minimum of 8 hours (and they will stay for 12 hours).

To Improve Your Earnings

- Bring specialized skills to the job. For example, if you have a nursing background, you could offer night nanny care for children with medical conditions. and charge a higher hourly rate.

- Offer nighttime services at your home instead of on site, and bring on some additional children. It would be a lower price for each parent, but you could earn more by watching several children at once.

Necessary Skills

To make this job work, you probably need the following:

- Lots of patience! The folks I know who used a night nanny had extra complications like twins or colic, so you need to be prepared to deal with this.

- Good baby skills and lots of different methods up your sleeve to deal with potential issues. You may want to take a class if your experience is only with your own children rather than at a daycare or similar center.

What You Need to Get Started

Experience or training with babies would be the most important requirement.

Making it Work with Kids

Generally, you won't be able to bring your children along, so this is one case where you'll need to arrange for a spouse, family member, or friend to care for your children while you are on duty.

Potty Training

What Is It?

Potty training can be difficult, and only happens once with each child, so parents don't often have much experience in this area. A potty trainer would come to the house, most likely for a weekend, for a 2 or 3-day potty training marathon and assist the family in teaching the child this skill. There might also be classes or in-home sessions to teach the parents how to best toilet train their children.

Economics

You will need to determine the acceptable pricing in your local area. In general, this would be either an hourly rate to offer assistance or some sort of fixed rate where you are with the family a certain number of hours on specific days during the process.

To Improve Your Earnings

Offer group classes to parents on how to potty train, rather than doing the work in person.

Necessary Skills

To make this job work, you probably need the following:

Great patience! This can be a slow and frustrating process in some cases.

A lot of tricks, tips and skills around potty training. If you don't have a lot of experience in this area (for instance, you've potty trained multiple children at a daycare), you should probably get several books on the subject from the library and put together your own reference sheet of ideas and tips.

What You Need to Get Started
To get started, you really just need your first customer. Once you're ready to go, you may want to offer to help a friend or relative for free so they can serve as a reference customer.

Making it Work with Kids
Generally, you won't be able to bring your children along, so this is one case where you'll need to arrange for a spouse, family member, or friend to care for your children while you are on duty.

10

Pets

Lots of people have pets, which makes pet-related services in demand, especially in urban areas where they may be closed up in a small apartment all day while the owner is at work. People also often need pet care while out of town and may need help with grooming or errands.

Here are some different pet-related businesses you might consider; some of them pay surprisingly well once you get them up and running.

Dog Walker

What Is It?
A dog walker comes and takes the dog(s) out for a walk/ potty break in the middle of the day while the family is at work. In urban areas I've lived in, it's common to see a dog walker pick up various dogs in a neighborhood and walk them around the neighborhood for 30 minutes or so. In a suburban area, it might make sense to pick up several dogs in your vehicle and transport them all to a local dog park for a run around. Dog walkers are also often available for pet sitting when the owners are away.

Economics
A professional dog walker told me that those who consider themselves professionals limit their walks to six dogs at a time. In my local area, dog walks are $10 per day per dog; this will obviously vary, so you'll need to check out your area. It's likely more in urban spots.

If we assume the dogs you walk are fairly close to each other geographically and that you will keep them all out for 30 minutes, you can walk six dogs per hour (this allows for 15 minutes on each end to pick up and then drop off the pets). At $10 each, this is $60 per hour. If you work partial days while your children are at school or otherwise occupied, you can potentially earn $180 per day in three hours, which is $900 a week or $46,800 per year (assuming no time off for holidays; likely actual earnings will be lower due to breaks). This is still quite a good income, especially for a part time option.

To Improve Your Earnings

- Increase the dogs per walk or the walks per day

- Reduce travel time between houses so you can fit in an additional walk in the same amount of time

- Add on services you could perform as part of the walking service. For example, you could walk and feed a pet twice a day while the owner is away, or you could trim the pet's toenails or take them by the groomer on a monthly basis.

Necessary Skills

To make this job work, you probably need the following:

- Excellent skills in handling dogs, including an understanding of dog psychology and different dog equipment available for dogs that are harder to walk.

- Insurance in case a dog is hurt, or hurts someone while you are responsible for it.

- If you are in a suburban or rural area, a way to transport dogs in your vehicle, such as crates in the back of a large SUV. In an urban area, you may be able to walk between houses to pick up your charges.

What You Need to Get Started

- Check with your insurance company to make sure you're covered in case a dog is hurt or hurts someone while you are responsible for them.

- A written contract to have your customers sign, which gives their contact information, gives you permission to take their dog to the vet if there's an emergency (have them provide vet information), and defines the cost per walk, how often and when you will walk their dog, how you will obtain entry to their premises (key under the mat?), and how often you'll be paid (monthly in advance?).

- A comfortable pair of walking shoes!

Making it Work with Kids

This is a business that works well with most kids. If your children are younger, you can take the dogs to a dog park to run around while your child sits in the stroller or plays in the playground. Older children can walk the pets with you.

House/Pet Sitter

What Is It?

Taking care of pets while people are out of town. You can add a layer of professionalism by keeping a brief log or journal of your activities, such as the times the dogs ate or anything interesting that happened during your walk or playtime.

Economics

In my area "friends of friends" pet sitters are about $20 per day; professionals about $30 per day. This usually includes coming by the house twice per day to feed the dogs, a walk or some time spent playing with the dogs, feeding of any other animals (fish, for example), and bringing in the mail and newspaper.

To Improve Your Earnings

- Offer additional services while you are there, such as giving the dog a bath or a nail clip

- Offer an add-on service when you are already at the house, for example dog walking or dog poop cleanup.

Necessary Skills

To make this job work, you probably need the following:

- Insurance. People will usually want you to be bonded before you have the run of their home, unless they already know you personally

- Good organizational skills to make sure you keep good track of mealtimes, walks, etc.

What You Need to Get Started

Once you've made sure you're covered in case you are accused of theft or negligence - just a customer! Spread the word via email or Facebook, post online in any groups you belong to, and put an ad on craigslist.org to try to get those first few customers.

Making it Work with Kids

As long as your children are well-behaved and use appropriate care around pets, you should have no issues bringing them along. In fact, they can even assist with feeding the pets and bringing in the mail!

Grooming/Errands

What Is It?
Taking dogs to appointments such as at the groomer, taking the pet to a dog wash and grooming them, providing grooming services at the client's home, or doing pet-related errands such as picking up dog food.

Economics
Running errands will probably just be an hourly fee; $10 - $30 an hour is the likely rate. If you provide the grooming services, you can increase the pricing a bit for your expertise. In my area, a nail clip is $10 to $20 (and takes about a minute!) and a bath/brush job is $40 - $60. You can call local groomers for comparable rates or pick up a rate sheet at a local PetSmart that offers grooming services.

To Improve Your Earnings
- Offer additional services, such as dog walking or pet sitting.

- Learn how to do some specialty grooming, such as getting dogs ready for show, formal poodle clips, etc.

Necessary Skills
To make this job work, you probably need the following:

- Reliable transportation that includes a way to safely transport pets

- Insurance in case a dog is hurt or hurts someone while you are responsible for them.

What You Need to Get Started

Once you've made sure you are covered in case you are accused of theft or negligence - just a customer! Spread the word via email or Facebook, post online in any groups you belong to, and put an ad on craigslist.org to try to get those first few customers.

Making it Work with Kids

Your kids can ride along as you run to the pet store or groomers, so this one should work well with children.

Pooper Scooper

What Is It?

Hey, you've heard the theory that the best way to make money is to do something other people don't want to do, right? Well this is one of those businesses. As a pooper-scooper, you drive to people's homes, usually once a week, and clean up waste in their yard from their pet(s).

Economics

In my area, cleaning up after a single dog is $8.25 per week and additional dogs add to the weekly cost at $3.50 each. The actual cleanup job takes about five minutes a yard, but the economics depend heavily on how close together your customers are. Initially, you would want to focus on a single geographic area, or perhaps have a different area for each day of the week and use a map to plan your route to minimize time and gas usage. If we assume you need 10 minutes to get to the next location, then each yard takes 10 minutes of travel time plus five minutes to clean, or 15 minutes per yard. You can do 4 yards per hour. At the $8.25 minimum per house, your earnings would be $8.25/yard times 4 yards/hour, or $33 an hour.

To Improve Your Earnings

- get yards even closer together to reduce travel time

- charge more for the service

- emphasize multi-dog homes since the cleaning time won't change much for the additional pickup

Necessary Skills

To make this job work, you probably need the following:

- A love (or at least a like!) of dogs

- The ability to do something kind of gross if it brings in income to your family

- Reliability - your customers depend on you to come when you say you'll be there. A couple of no-shows and they'll hire someone else.

What You Need to Get Started

To get started in this business, you'll need:

- scooper equipment. There are sets available at pet stores with a small long-handled rake and long-handled dustpan. Carry a small trash can lined with a plastic bag and you have a place to put the waste that you scoop. Gloves would also be a good addition, both to help keep your hands clean and to prevent blisters. You might consider some lightweight medical-type gloves under a pair of heavy leather work gloves.

- a supply of plastic bags

- a way to disinfect your equipment between yards to avoid carrying disease from one house to another. A scooper in my area says, "Before and after each yard we visit, we use several disinfectants on all of our equipment. This includes a Parvo-killing anti-microbial as well as a bleach solution." (from http://www.hanlyshounds.com/). You can set up your trunk to disinfect and transport your equipment from house to house. You will probably want to have a large, heavy tarp inside your trunk so that if you want to use it for another purpose later, it will be sanitary enough.

- insurance in case you cause some sort of harm to their pets. It would also be good to be bonded. Contact your insurance agent to find out the cost of this.

Making it Work with Kids

Probably the only way to make this work if you have kids home full time is to have them ride along and wait in the vehicle. You risk issues of them being bitten or hurt in a stranger's yard, and younger kids may not be very sanitary about cleaning up waste. Luckily, each stop will only take a few minutes. With a small DVD player, you can entertain your little one while you run in.

11

Selling Products Online

Does the vision of you strolling through stores locating outstanding bargains and then selling them online from home inspire you? Or, do you love to make your beautiful handcrafted quilts and would like to earn some money from your creativity? If so, an online products business may be perfect for you!

If you want to create a business selling products online, you have two primary issues to solve to get started:

1. What are you going to sell?

2. Where are you going to sell it?

We'll cover both of these topics in the next sections.

Finding Goods to Sell

For those of you who are creating goods to sell, this part is easy. You'll want to focus your efforts on getting your basic materials as inexpensively as possible (but still meeting your quality standards of course) and look for ways to make your items more unique or alternatively easier to create quickly so you can generate more sales from a given amount of time.

The rest of this section is for those who aren't making items to sell, but instead want to purchase existing products and resell them.

In my time selling on eBay, I've found goods to sell in a lot of different ways: wholesalers, garage sales, thrift stores, outgrown items from my own kids, eBay trading assistant, and purchases from stores. I've found my absolute best results were with store purchases. Here are some advantages:

- brand new merchandise, so very low incidence of unhappy customers, missed problems with the clothing, etc.

- If an item doesn't sell, I can generally return it to that store for a full refund! Keep your receipts - and know your store policies - because this is a huge advantage.

I've purchased wholesale lots before, and although the per item price sounded favorable for major department store shelf pulls,- when I got the items, there were many nice things, and (my favorite!) in one case, 30+ orange plaid short-sleeve button up men's shirts by Tommy Hilfiger. Buying retail means you get to pick out exactly what you think you can sell, rather than getting random items.

The secret to making income with reselling purchases is to buy them at the right (low) price! It takes some dedication to get this started, as you need to select some appropriate stores and visit them regularly (I would suggest at least weekly) to put together a good clearance schedule for that particular store. You can also talk to store employees and get some guidance on when new markdowns occur.

My personal guideline is that I only purchase items I believe I can sell for three times what I'm paying for them. That means with rare exceptions (such as hot toys found in a store when they are sold out most other places), I only purchase items on clearance for at least 70% off. The item is at 30% of its original retail price, so I can mark up price paid x3 and be at 90% of original retail price. That also gives me the opportunity to discount items that don't sell promptly and still make money!

In addition, there are costs associated with listing, selling, accepting payments via PayPal, and shipping the goods you sell. Due to those various costs, I only will get items I can sell for at least $10. That's the cutoff point where it makes sense to me to take the time to list. I also look for items where I can purchase multiple identical items (saves time in preparing the listing), and more expensive items I believe will sell (then one listing can result in a much higher profit).

To find those sorts of deals, you need a lot of patience. It's also best to have some storage and some money you can invest into inventory, since you will find the best deals at end of season sales but may not be able to sell the items for a good profit until that season rolls around the next year. In my years of selling on eBay, I've found summer clothing sells best April through June, fall school clothing in August, and winter clothing August through October. New items, especially holiday dresses and items appropriate for Christmas presents, sell well in November. There's also another brief period of great sales in toys and electronics in early January, as people spend any cash they received for the things they wished they'd gotten. Business-related items seem to sell year round, as do many collectibles and electronic items.

Where to Sell Online

The first decision to ponder when deciding where to sell online is whether to develop your own website or market your products in existing marketplaces. My experience is that it takes a fair bit of time and effort to develop a traffic stream to your website and you need significant traffic to generate sales. Unless you have an existing website with targeted traffic that might be interested in your product or a specialized avenue such as the chance to sell exclusively on an existing high-traffic and targeted website, I'd recommend you take advantage of the marketplaces already in place that have significant traffic. There are four different places I'd recommend you consider for selling your products online: Amazon, EBay, Etsy and craigslist. I'll discuss each of these in turn.

Amazon (http://www.amazon.com)

Amazon is an excellent marketplace for selling new or used books, movies, and software. There's also a good market for homeschool items and office supplies, and many children's items and toys - even last year's items - new or used. If you label and ship your items to an Amazon warehouse, they are eligible for free Prime shipping. Amazon Prime isa program where customers pay an annual fee and receive free 2-day shipping on all their orders of items shipped to them from an Amazon.com warehouse, which can increase your sales since it's a lower price to the customer due to the free shipping.

Getting Started

To get started, go to Amazon and click on the "Sell on Amazon" link at the bottom of the screen. It will take you to the area showing their current options. Currently, you can list items for free if you sell less than 40 per month (they take fees out of the selling price), or pay a monthly fee of $39.99 to sell more than 40 with lower fees for each sale. If you want to sell an item, the easiest way to do it is to do a search for the product on the Amazon website. Once it comes up, on the right side of the screen you'll see several boxes with information about purchasing new, purchasing used, or possibly trading in your copy. Then, right at the bottom and just above the site link symbols, you'll see a button that says "Have one to sell?" and a button that says "Sell on Amazon". Click on this button to get started.

Enter in your item's condition, a brief note describing the item, and specify where you will ship it from (an example: Purchased new, read once, like-new condition. Fast shipping from NV.), your price, and types of shipping you'll offer. Under shipping, the choice of "I want Amazon to ship and provide customer service for my items" requires you to label the item and ship it to an Amazon warehouse as part of their "Fulfilled by Amazon" program. If you have a lot of items to sell, this program is highly recommended as your items will be eligible for free 2-day shipping to many of Amazon's customers which will increase your sales; otherwise, it's easiest to ship yourself.

Fulfilled by Amazon:

With the Fulfilled by Amazon program, you label and ship your items to Amazon and they store them in their warehouse. When the customer purchases one of your items, Amazon ships it to the customer and credits your seller account for the selling price, less their fees. Items in their warehouse are eligible for free super saver shipping and free 2-day prime shipping, which increases sales.

There are storage fees for items in their warehouse, so it's best to send them items you anticipate will sell in a reasonable amount of time. There's also some time involved in the labeling process and you will pay to have the items shipped to their warehouse. This can be an excellent program if you have a lot of items to sell, as you can take the time to label them in bulk, then send them in and they will handle the products from there.

If you have just a few items, it will likely be easier for you to list them for sale and then ship them yourself when they sell.

EBay (http://www.ebay.com)

Think of this as the world's largest garage sale! People come to eBay looking for hard to find items, especially collectibles, and great deals. There are also a lot of people looking for educational items.

Successful eBay Listings

Here are some of your most important considerations when selling online at eBay:

Auction Titles

The title of your listing is extremely important, since that is how people will locate your item. Think about what you might type into a search engine to locate that particular item and try to include all those words in the title. Some specific things I include are:

- Brand name, if applicable

- Items included (console + 3 games; 6pc top pants)

- Color

- Size, if applicable

- NWT (stands for new with tag) or NEW, so people know it's a brand new item. Here are a few other acronyms that might be useful:

  NWOT = new without tag
  NIB = new in box
  NIP = new in package
  HTF = hard to find
  LN = like new

- a few features or differentiators. For clothing, I might include "appliqué" or "lace", for specialty items, "limited edition" or "hard to find", and toys may be "hot" or "sold out". So, "rare black edition" would generally get more interest than just "black".

Pictures

Pictures are also extremely important. It's much better to use a decent digital camera rather than your phone, since the picture will likely be much clearer. Try to eliminate distractions in the photo by having a neutral background (I have a tan sheet I lay on the carpet or on a table when I need a simple background) and not having extra items in the shot. One time on eBay, I saw a picture of children's clothing for sale, taken on a carpet surrounded by Cheerios. Don't do this! Crop the photo, using editing software if you need to, or be careful not to include extras in the picture. Make sure you have good light and the item(s) are laid out in an attractive fashion, so that the prospective buyer can see details of the and has the impression it's of high quality. Many people will buy your item by the photo alone, so take the necessary time to make sure it's top notch.

Auction Description

The description in the auction states exactly what's included (and if a common accessory or part is not included, it should clearly say so), and should try to answer all likely questions by including size, measurements, a description of any damage, etc. You don't want to highlight problems and scare people off, but the key to having happy customers is them getting exactly what they expect or perhaps something slightly nicer. Don't hide any flaws and make sure they know exactly what they are getting!

Pricing

Pricing is one of the toughest jobs you have. Ideally, a couple of bidders will really want your auction, will bid it up, and it won't matter how you've priced it, but that doesn't always happen. There are two types of prices on eBay: opening bid for auction items and Buy It Now for items that a customer can purchase any time they are willing to pay the set amount. You'll need to decide whether you want to encourage multiple bidders on your item through auction style or set a flat price anyone can pay.

Auction Style Pricing

There are two strategies you can use to set pricing. The first is to set your opening bid for the minimum you will accept for the item. This way, you know you will be happy if the item sells. Unfortunately, I've found that people who haven't sold many items on eBay yet are often unrealistic about what their used items are worth. Even NWT (new with tag) items may go for less than you paid for them. To get an idea of appropriate value, do a search on eBay of items like the one you're selling. When you get the search results, click on "search on closed auctions" to see recent auction results for items like yours. This will give you a good feeling for what your particular auction may fetch.

The second is to set a very low opening bid to get attention - say $.99. If you are concerned you might not get enough bids to be happy with your ending price, you can always set a reserve at the minimum you would be satisfied with to make sure it doesn't go too low. I've found that you will get lots more viewers with a low opening price, and in my opinion, you will get a higher ending price that way since more viewers generally equals more bidders. You only need two bidders who really want your item to get a high ending price!

Buy It Now Pricing

In terms of Buy It Now (BIN), here are some things to think about:

- If someone is interested in your item but BIN isn't available, they may go to another auction to buy it immediately

- On the other hand, if something is very popular, you may leave money on the table by allowing someone to BIN rather than compete via the auction process

- I personally like BIN since it puts money in my pocket faster! If you decide to use BIN in your auctions, I would suggest that you:

  - Set a high BIN price for popular items. Someone may BIN if they really want it, so you'll get a nice bonus on the auction, and if not, it will get the bidding process started sooner since a bid must be placed to remove the option of someone else Buying It Now.

  - Set a BIN price less than two times your opening bid for all other items. For example, if your opening bid price is $7.99, set a BIN of $15.00. I've found that with rare exceptions (like really hot products), a BIN more than two times the opening bid will not be taken.

Shipping:

You also need to include shipping prices in your listing. On eBay, if you provide the shipping weight of the item at the time you create the listing, eBay will automatically calculate shipping for your buyer based on their geographic location. To do this, you need to prepare the item for shipping, so make sure you have the right size box or envelope on hand, determine any extras you might need like bubble wrap or a plastic bag, and weigh and measure the whole thing. Then you'll have the needed information to let eBay calculate the correct shipping for you. I've lost money before when the shipping was more than I anticipated, so take this step seriously so you get the expected profit from your auctions. I have a small postal scale I purchased at the post office that I use to weigh my packages during my listings.

Getting Started

EBay has excellent tutorials to walk you through the process of selling items. Go to the eBay home page and click on "sell" in the upper right menu bar for the tutorials.

Etsy (http://www.etsy.com)

This site focuses exclusively on handmade items. If you have items you've made yourself, you will want to list them here. You may want to sell them on eBay as well, although the price points on Etsy tend to be higher.

Keys to Making it Work

You need top notch photos of your items on this site, so people really understand the quality of the items you're selling. Take the time to get great photos before you list your items for sale.

You also want to make sure your items are original and unique in some way. There's a lot of competition so make sure your items stand out in some fashion.

Be sure to keep good track of your production costs and time so you sell your items for enough to pay you for producing them! Calculate your hourly rate of pay from your goods at the price you anticipate selling them for, and make sure it's worthwhile for you to produce them.

Getting Started

Etsy has excellent tutorials to walk you through the process of selling items. Go to the Etsy home page and click on "sell" in the upper left menu bar for the tutorials.

Craigslist (http://www.craigslist.org)

Craigslist is a local marketplace and an excellent place to sell items too big or not worthwhile for shipping. Use it for large items like furniture and baby gear, or for lots of small items when you prefer not to have a garage sale.

It's important to have pictures on craigslist. Although they will allow you to list without them, you bring your odds of selling things way down when people can't see in advance what the item looks like.

Be prepared for a number of no-shows when people ask to come and see your items. I've found this to be a continual source of frustration to me with this site, though I sell enough items through it quickly and easily to just accept that it will happen frequently.

Once an item sells, please go ahead and remove the listing so no additional people will contact you about it.

Pricing on Craigslist

I find that about half the time I sell things on craigslist, people pay me the asking amount listed on the website, and the other half of the time, they make a lower offer. I generally set prices a little higher than the amount I'm willing to accept so I have room to negotiate for those who prefer to haggle.

Getting Started

The easiest way to get started on craigslist is to set up an account. Go to the craigslist website, and near the upper left, click on the "My Account" link. It will take you to a login screen. Near the bottom is a link to "Sign up for an account". You can list things without an account and the site will send you an email with a link to edit each listing, but with an account, you can log in and see all your open listings in a nice list.

To list something for sale, go to the home page and click on the "For Sale" link (near the middle). Once you're in the items for sale section you will see a "Post" link near the upper right of your screen; click on it and it will walk you through the process.

12

Selling Information Online

I've read a lot of guides to selling information online, tried a lot of things (and spent a lot of money!), and only made money when I wrote and sold my information through Amazon (http://www.amazon.com). I personally use Create Space (http://www.createspace.com - an Amazon-owned company) as my hard copy publisher, and upload my books to Kindle Direct Publishing (https://kdp.amazon.com/) so they are available for sale on the Kindle. I have not uploaded my books in Nook format at Barnes & Noble as I currently have my Kindle books enrolled in the KDP Select program - more on that later :)

Your first step is to actually write a book, so we'll cover that first in this guide. Then I'll talk about publishing your book, i.e. making it available for sale.

Writing a Book to Sell Online

Your First Step: Finding Time to Write

The very first thing you need to do if you're going to write a book to sell is make time to write it! I suggest you figure out a specific time each day so it won't be pushed off by the mountain of other things you have to do. I've found I can't spend more than about an hour at a time on my projects, and some days it's only 15 minutes.

Focus on spending time working on your project, even if it doesn't sound like fun and you feel out of ideas. Once you sit down and start thinking, you can likely come up with some step to take that day towards your end goal - maybe it's writing, maybe it's developing an outline of a new book or chapter, maybe it's doing some research for your topic.

Focus on the time rather than the entire project. If I think about what's left in a project, I tend to get overwhelmed and don't want to do anything! Instead, focus on how you can best spend the next 15 minutes in moving your project a step forward.

Picking A Topic

I personally write non-fiction guides, and have read before that they generally sell better than fiction works. However, that sort of thinking all goes out the window if you write the next *Harry Potter* or *Twilight*, so I'm going to suggest you... do what you like best and are good at!

In non-fiction, it's good to start with a list of things you know a lot about or would like to know a lot more about, and then pick your specific option based on both willingness to write a whole bunch about that topic and interest from potential readers. I judge interest with the Google AdWords Keyword tool. These things periodically change URLs, so just enter that into a search engine to find it. In the "word or phrase" box, enter in various things you are considering writing about, with each topic or idea on a separate line. Then fill in the crazy letters in the human check box and click on "search". The tool will return many similar phrases and will tell you how many global searches there were on each phrase in the prior month. This will give you a good idea on the amount of interest in your topic. You don't necessarily need a super high demand topic, as those will have more competition also, but make sure it's something of interest to prospective buyers. Once you've narrowed down to a specific topic, enter it into the keyword tool by itself, and read through all the similar phrases Google provides to determine your best keywords (use them later in the title of your book) and specific sub-topics you may want to focus on or include in your guide.

In fiction, you will not need to do this step - just get going on your book!

Writing a Description and Optimizing the Title

I use Google to optimize my titles. The basic idea is that you want a title that both gives the prospective reader a good idea of what the book is about, and that includes several key words that a buyer might type into Amazon or another search engine to locate information about the topic you're writing about.

Do a search to locate the Google AdWords keyword tool. These things move periodically, so I'm not including a link here!

In the top box for "word or phrase", type in words or phrases relating to your key topic to figure out which have the most searches. For example, for this book I might have typed "work at home" and "home business". Each search phrase or term goes on a separate line, so hit the enter key in between them. Type in the spam checker info, then click on "search".

To come up with the best words or phrases for your book, put yourself in the buyer's shoes. If they really wanted a book exactly like yours, what sort of things would they search for to try to find it? Once you find a few search terms that fit with your book and have a high number of searches, you have found it!

At the lower part of your screen, you will see each of your words and phrases and the number of monthly searches for each. This will allow you to optimize your title based on the key words most often used to look for information on the subject you're writing about.

I use both title and subtitle for my books, and put the most important key phrase in the title in case it's cut off in some search engines. For example, the name of my Spanish kids' book is "Lightning fast Spanish for Kid and Families: Learn Spanish, speak Spanish, teach kids Spanish - quick as a flash, even if you don't speak a word now". My number one key phrase was "Spanish for kids". I also wanted to include "learn Spanish, speak Spanish, teach kids Spanish", plus have a catchy title that would capture the interest of people looking for books of this type. You can also see that the less important part of the subtitle - "quick as a flash, even if you don't speak a word now"

- is at the end, so if a particular search engine truncated my title, the key words would still come up.

Writing the Book Abstract

I'd suggest you write up an abstract, or brief description designed to get the attention of potential readers up front. Then, when writing your book, you can periodically refer back to it to make sure your book is meeting the needs you identified in the abstract.

Start by writing down the problem your book would solve for the reader. For my Spanish book described above, it was "a way for moms to teach Spanish to their kids that doesn't take a lot of time and effort for the mom and works even if they are not bilingual". A book about Abraham Lincoln might cover "all about the life of Abraham Lincoln", or "how Abraham Lincoln really died". A fiction book might be "a great comedy escape for those who love humor, vampires, and supernatural themes".

You'll then write down what your book will do for the reader in a bit more detail, and rewrite it into a concise, short summary of what they will get out of your book. This is the marketing description you'll later use when publishing your book, so it will appear on book sellers' websites.

Here was the final result for the Spanish book:

> No time to learn Spanish? Want to teach your children but don't speak Spanish yourself? Lightning-Fast Spanish helps you incorporate Spanish into your everyday activities, so you learn while doing the things you already do!

You'll teach your children Spanish the same way you taught them English - by interacting with them as you do daily activities. No need to set aside extra time in your busy schedule, and no need to speak Spanish yourself - with this unique program, you both learn as you go. You'll be amazed at how quickly you see results!

If you want to get your family speaking Spanish fast - this book is for you!

Lightning-Fast Spanish is:
* Built around every day situations - no need to set aside special time, and you will use your new language the first day!
* Ready to use with phonetic pronunciation included - no current Spanish knowledge needed!
* Fun and easy to start!

Outlining The Book

Before you start writing specific sections of your book, do an outline and plan what you're going to include or the main things that will happen in each chapter. Many people will go one step further and break down the main points or activities within each chapter as well.

Once you have the broad outline, it's time to go section by section and start writing. This makes sure everything you write supports the overall book you want to provide at the end.

Writing The Book

This can be the tough part. One of the keys here is to keep going! Figure out what time you will sit down each day and how long you will spend. You may not feel motivated when you sit down, but you need to have the discipline to open a section and start typing or it will never be finished!

Try not to edit as you go, as this will slow you down. Instead, get everything down on paper and once the section or chapter is complete, you can go back at another session and edit it or wait until you have rough information down for your entire book and then do a large editing effort all at once.

Creating A Cover

When I originally published my language books, I didn't feel I had enough money to have a cover professionally done, so I created one myself. After several months and releasing the book in several other languages, I went back and hired a cover designer to create professional covers for all the books. It made an immediate impact on sales and the higher sales stayed consistently higher. It was definitely worth the money I spent, since the sales continue on month after month into the future. I personally think the most important aspects of having your book sell are a good looking professional cover, good customer reviews (this requires a well-written, well-edited book to achieve), and an abstract that catches the attention of the readers you are trying to reach. So, don't skimp on the cover!

To find a cover designer, I posted my project on Elance (http://www.elance.com). The person I now work with is a professional artist in the publishing industry who does book covers on the side.

Editing

One of the biggest complaints about self-published books is the lack of editing - in other words, the number of typos, mistakes, or poorly written sections in the book.

If you do have a budget for editing, it's money well spent, since it will help you get the reviews you need to sell more books. If not, you can still find ways to edit your work. First, if you are a good writer, you can probably put your project aside for a few days, then return to it and catch many errors. Second, you may be able to find a friend or two who will be willing to read your draft and provide corrections to grammar and spelling and propose areas needing improvement. Third, you can join Scribophile (http://www.scribophile.com), which is a website where authors post sections of their work in progress and receive editorial comments from other writers. You have to build up "karma points" by editing others' work in order to post your own, so you do need some time available for this method. Fourth, you could hire someone less expensive who is a good writer. For example, a college student getting some sort of writing or literature degree and who has excellent writing skills might be willing to review and edit your document for a low hourly rate.

Hard Copy or Kindle?

Personally, I do both! So far, I find I sell about 60% hard copies, 40% Kindle version, so both have been worth doing for me.

Pricing

Pricing is always a difficult decision. I'd suggest you do some searches at online booksellers and look at the pricing of a lot of books similar to yours to make your pricing decision.

- You may want to make your book the same price as similar books available from large publishers, or you may want to be less expensive.

- You may want both the hard copy and Kindle to have the same pricing, or you may want the Kindle version to be less expensive (this is common).

- If you have a series of books, many authors make the first book or two in the series much less expensive in the Kindle version (since there are minimal fixed costs to cover) to get the reader "hooked" so they come back and purchase the rest of the series at full price.

Both Kindle Direct and Create Space have royalty calculators built into their system that you can use while loading your book to determine your royalty per copy sold based on different retail prices.

Preparing and Uploading Hard Copy (Expanded Distribution – Maybe)

Once your book is finalized, it's time to get it ready for sale! I use Create Space (http://www.createspace.com) for my hard copies. It's integrated with the Amazon.com website and books are printed on demand and shipped via Amazon's delivery services, including free SuperSaver and Prime shipping. There is another printer I've heard a lot about called Lightning Source, and it sounds like there may be some pricing advantages. I'd encourage you to look into it if you are interested, and to consider the book "POD for Profit: More on the NEW Business of Self-Publishing", or "How to Publish Your Books With Online Book Marketing and Print on Demand by Lightning Source" by Aaron Shepard (Shepard Publications; 2010), if you'd like to use this method.

Here, I'll just discuss Create Space. Here are the basic steps to getting your book ready to upload into the Create Space system:

1. Create an account at Create Space.

2. Click on "Add new title" near the upper left .

3. Fill in your title and select "book". If you are new, I'd suggest you choose "guided setup". It will walk you through the process of adding in your subtitle, author information, book size, and book description (this is the book abstract you developed earlier).

4. You will need to upload your cover file or create your own using the Cover Creator program. In Cover Creator, there are a number of previously created templates and you just choose one and have it put on your title, author and back cover information.

5. To get your book file ready to upload, I have written some basic instructions, and detailed tutorials are on the Create Space website. However, if these don't make sense to you, I'll suggest you find someone with a lot of experience with word processing programs to walk you through the first time!

   - You'll need your book in a word processing program. I use Microsoft Word and am assuming your program has the same functionality.

- Change your page size in the word processing program to match the book size you selected during the Create Space setup.

- At the beginning of the file, create your title page and copyright page (pull a book off your shelf and take a look at the beginning to see what I'm talking about). The simplest copyright statement is just "© 2012 by [insert your name], All rights reserved". You might also want acknowledgements; if so, put those in now.

- After the information just discussed and before the first page of your introduction or first chapter, insert a table of contents. In Microsoft Word, if you highlight each chapter heading and set the format to "Heading 1", you can then have it automatically create a table of contents for you using the "References - Table of Contents" menu command (this is MS Word 2007; location in other versions may vary).

- Add in a header and/or footer if you like. Page numbering generally appears in the footer.

- Set up your document so you can view two pages at a time, and go through and fix the pagination so that chapters all start on a new sheet of paper. If you are viewing your document two pages at a time, all new chapters should start on the left.

- Suppress headers and footers on any completely blank pages. For example, any blank pages needed to make a new chapter start on a new sheet of paper.

- If it all looks good, save your document into .pdf format (in MS Word 2007, click on the logo in the upper left, then "Save As" and "PDF").

- Use a PDF viewer like Adobe Reader to make sure your document is the correct size (maybe even print a page to verify) and looks good.

- Then, you are ready to upload the file into Create Space.

6. Whew! Once your interior file is uploaded, you'll save your progress and move on to selecting distribution channels. I'd suggest you select all available. You will have one choice to make - if you pay $25, your book can be available to other retailers and libraries as well. I personally pay this on most of my books, and it's been worth doing as I sell a few through those channels each month.

7. Once you've completed the forms, you can submit your book for review. Create Space staff will make sure it's ready to print and notify you when it's available for sale. Once it's ready, it will take a few days to appear on the Amazon website. If you choose the expanded distribution upgrade, it will take a couple of weeks to appear on other websites.

Preparing and Uploading – Kindle Version

If you've already loaded your book into Create Space, you will have the option of listing it for sale in Kindle version on their website. Alternatively, you can load it via the Kindle Direct Publishing (https://kdp.amazon.com/) website (this is the method I've used). They have a good tutorial on exactly how to format your file for upload. Here's a super short version:

- Start with your original book file in MS Word with the header, footer, title page, other front information, and table of contents in it.

- Make sure your file is set up to have each chapter start on a new page.

- Next, you'll want to add in a couple of bookmarks. A Kindle reader has the option to *"Go To"* the cover image, beginning of the book and the Table of Contents of your book, by using a command on their device. The specific information they see when they use this command is defined by what are known as "Guide Items." If you upload a cover image, the cover Guide Item will be set automatically. To define the other Guide Items, follow the steps below:

  For the Beginning:
  Place the cursor where you want the book to start, click on "Insert > Bookmark." In the "Bookmark name:" field, type "Start" (without the quotes) and click "Add."

  For the Table of Contents:
  Place the cursor at the beginning of the first entry in the Table of Contents. Click on "Insert > Bookmark." In the

"Bookmark name:" field, type "TOC" (without the quotes) and click "Add."

- Now you are ready to upload your book.

- Once you set up an account with Kindle Direct, you will have a button for "Create New Title" near the upper left. Once you click on that, you will need to fill in your title, author and book description information, add some keywords people might search on to find your book, and upload your cover file (front cover only) plus your book file (in MS Word).

- After you "Save and Continue" the information on the first page, you'll be taken to a second page to select where you book will be sold and it's pricing. Once this information is entered and saved, your book will go into review status.

Once your book is uploaded, it should be available for sale in 1 to 2 days on the Amazon web site.

Getting Reviews on Amazon

Once your book is available for sale, your next crucial task is to get reviews posted so prospective readers know what to expect if they buy your book.

Usually, the first place to start is with people you know. Ask them if they would be willing to read your book and post a review.

A second option is to join Book Blogs (http://bookblogs.ning.com/). This is a group of writers and bloggers, and some of the ongoing forums are places to post requests for book reviews. You can find people to do book giveaways here as well. This is usually combined with a review. Their readers can enter in a drawing for a free copy once they read about the book.

Another excellent way to get reviews is to offer free review copies to bloggers. I've found they will read the book (sometimes it takes a while), post a review on their blog, and then happily repost their review on Amazon if you request it.

To locate bloggers interested in reading your book, you can:

- Do a Google search on "blogs" + "[fill in the topic of your book here]", to locate blogs that might be interested in your book. Look through the blog of each potential reviewer before you contact them, to make sure they do reviews and that their focus seems compatible with your book. If so, contact them (there is generally a contact list on their blog page) and ask them if they would be interested. You can sweeten it by offering a hard copy (most prefer this to an electronic version) and by offering a second copy as a giveaway for their site.

- Do a Google search for "largest blogs" + "[fill in the topic of your book here]", to locate lists of blogs with high readership. You can also specifically check the various lists at Blog Rank http://www.invesp.com/blog-rank.

- Go to Business2Blogger (http://business2blogger.com/) to locate bloggers interested in your project. On this site, you will pay for contact information for blogs you select, but it will save you a lot of time researching. Once you set up an account, you will post an ad for your project, such as "Seeking Bloggers to review language book" and write about what you are hoping to find, such as "I'm looking for 5 bloggers to review my new book "XXX". I'll provide a hard copy for review, plus set aside a second copy for a giveaway if you like. Here's a description of my book: XXX". Interested bloggers will respond to you and the response list will include various metrics on their web site rank, number of readers, etc. You will need to pay for contact information for the bloggers you select; base price is $5 per blogger with discounts if you purchase packages. After you purchase their information, you'll correspond with them directly to coordinate the review and giveaway.

Website/Facebook/Twitter/Blog

Setting up any or all of these methods of keeping in touch with readers and potential future readers can help increase your sales. If you do set them up, provide your various links to any bloggers who are going to review your book. They will generally include some links in their post so their readers can find or follow you, and may also be willing to give extra entries in a giveaway for readers who sign up for your blog, tweets, Facebook posts, etc.

If you're going to blog, I've read a lot on this topic and the consensus from those who do it seems to be that you should be sure to blog on topics of interest to your prospective readers.

There are two options for this:

1. Do a profile of the people you believe will be interested in your book - their age, occupation, interests, etc. - and then

create a list of topics you believe would also interest them, and use it as a guideline for your blog posts.

2. Write on your books specifically - for example, post occasional short stories using your main characters, or post an excerpt from your new book, or post additional information about your characters that is not generally available, such as a story from their childhood. This allows your readers to bond more closely with the characters you write about.

Author Page, Linking Editions, Adding a Blog and Twitter Feed

Once your book is available for sale on Amazon.com, you'll be able to set up an author page on their website. Visit Author Central at https://authorcentral.amazon.com/ to set this up. It will allow you to post a picture, biographical information, link all your books together to show up on your author page, and add links to your Twitter or blog accounts so that your posts automatically show up on your author page.

Other Ways to Spread the Word

One other promotional idea to consider is the Amazon.com KDP Select Program. If you are selling your books in Kindle version, you'll have the option of joining this program on the Bookshelf tab of the Kindle Direct Publishing website at https://kdp.amazon.com/.

In this program:

- Customers who are Amazon Prime members can borrow any books in the program for free, up to 1 per month

- The author of the book that is borrowed receives a payment from a fund that Amazon creates each month. Recent months have paid a little over $2.00 per borrow.

- Authors then have the opportunity to make their book available to all Amazon Kindle customers for free up to 5 days per quarter. This sounds like a strange opportunity - give my book away free? - but if a lot of people download your book while it's free, it will improve your position in the Amazon search rankings which in turn should increase sales of your book in the weeks after the giveaway.

Your greatest chance of a big jump in sales from doing a free promotion comes from one of the websites and blogs that lists recommended free books of the day posts your book in their guide. They are generally looking for popular books with a number of positive reviews, so you'll want to build up some sales and interest plus have at least five positive reviews before you try this.

I've also found that it's much more effective to make my books free on the weekend. There seems to be a lot less competition on those days.

One other consideration is that if your book is enrolled in KDP Select, you cannot offer it for sale in electronic format on any other website. Specifically, this means you can't upload it in Nook format to Barnes & Noble. Keep this in mind when making your final decision.

Wrapping It Up

Whew! You've made it to the end! If you've made it this far, you should have a plan for generating income that you are implementing step by step. Keep going, you can do it! At the beginning of a plan or project, the things that need to happen can seem insurmountable, but if you take some action (no matter how small) every day, you'll one day find you have the business you dreamed of back when you started this guide.

Circle back to the chapter on Your Income Plan and review your income matrix now that you have lots of new ideas. Complete your matrix, build your list of action steps, and get started on your business today! Then keep going, step by step... take some action and build your dream of making money from home - with kids!

www.ingramcontent.com/pod-product-compliance
Lightning Source LLC
Chambersburg PA
CBHW061508180526
45171CB00001B/88